Creating the New American School

A Principal's Guide to School Improvement

Richard DuFour
Robert Eaker

National Educational Service
Bloomington, Indiana   1992

Cover Design by Bryan Thatcher

Printed in the United States of America
ISBN 1-879639-17-3

recycled paper

Dedication

To Jewel Eaker, my mother; Star, my wife; Carrie and Robin, my children; and in memory of Raymond Eaker, my father. R.E.

To Susan and Matthew. R.D.

Acknowledgements

We wish to thank Thelma Sloan, Nancy McPherron, and Laura Lentz for their assistance in the preparation of the multiple drafts of the manuscript. We both owe a special debt to Dr. Jerry Bellon who has acted as a mentor and friend throughout our careers. We recognize and appreciate the special men and women of Adlai Stevenson High School in Lake County, Illinois, whose professionalism and dedication have helped to create an environment in which the ideas presented in this book could flourish.

Finally, our gratitude goes to our wives, Susan DuFour and Star Eaker, for their support and encouragement during the many months that we were preoccupied with writing this book.

Table of Contents

Foreword

Public schools have been the target of reform and improvement initiatives for several decades: innovation in the 1960's, accountability and improvement in the 1970's. The themes have changed as have the sponsors. At various times, impetus for change has come from local, state, and federal levels of government, as well as from within the education profession itself. The 1980's version of the ongoing series of reforms featured a national commission, state commissions, and legislation from Alaska to Florida, as well as a variety of programs sponsored at the local level.

Reform movements are complicated events. Each has several interested audiences with different agendas. One of these audiences is composed of policy-makers, policy-watchers, and citizens at-large. This group is most interesteed in the wider issues of reform: the recommendations of commissions, new legislation, and the commitment and concern of top officials. Another audience includes the citizens and parents in specific communities. While interested in the larger reform scene, these spectators focus their attention on their own school board, superintendent, principals, and teachers. They want to be reassured that their schools are either excellent or in the process of becoming so. A third audience, relatively uninterested in the drama, is a hard-minded crowd of analysts and academics — critics who want some tangible evidence that schools are better now than before all the activity began. They are waiting in the wings until reviews, research, and other evidence are accumulated and broadcast.

Amidst all of these diverse audiences is a seasoned, tired, and wary group of players — teachers and administrators. Many have been through all this before. They know their business. They are acutely aware that much of what the reformers want from them is already being delivered. They also see in reform programs suggestions that they already know are needed. And they know that some elements of the proposed reform could seriously harm education if they were put into practice.

The superintendents, principals, and teachers who are asked to improve the schools often are unsure of exactly how to proceed. Not only does each audience want something different, but there also is a cacophony of voices suggesting how it should be done differently. Some experts advocate the adoption of specific characteristics or attributes; others suggest that schools should emulate coroporations; still others outline specific strategies for improvement.

What can we legitimately expect from the 1980's reform efforts? If history is our guide, the outcome is fairly certain. Very little of any significance in schools will change. If we are fortunate, the activity itself will reaffirm our faith and confidence in our educational institutions. In many cases, thoughtful educators will use the reform initiatives as an opportunity to revitalize or refurbish outmoded patterns and practices. But when all the dust settles, a fundamental law will once again be reaffirmed. Human organizations are built, rebuilt, and remodeled from within. Raw materials and motivation can be imported from outside, but the actual work will be done by those on the premises. They need a foundation, an architectural design, and the tools to accomplish the job.

This book provides the ideas and tools that teachers and administrators need to respond to external mandates for reform. The authors have borrowed from several disciplines that are typically treated independently. They stress of building from within rather than importing from outside. They offer options without imposing prescriptions. Instead of offering abstract theories, the authors recognize that the practitioners themselves have the knowledge of how to proceed and build on their craft.

The reform movement of the 1990's provides a rare opportunity for education practitioners. They have a mandate to broadcast their virtues, revitalize tired practices, relabel some strengths, and alter some weaknesses. Books like this will help them augment their own intuition with some general ideas and principles.

Terry Deal
Vanderbilt University

Introduction

In April of 1983, the National Commission on Excellence in Education captured national attention with its grim assessment of education in the United States. In its report, entitled *A Nation at Risk*, the commission argued that the national security of the United States was in peril because of sub-standard education in its public schools. The commission made frequent references to "decline," "deficiencies," "threats," "risks," "afflictions," and "plight." The opening paragraphs of the report set the tone:

> Our nation is at risk. Our once unchallenged pre-eminence in commerce, industry, science, and technological innovation is being overtaken by competitors throughout the world. . . . The educational foundations of our society are presently being eroded by a rising tide of mediocrity that threatens our very future as a nation and a people. . . . If an unfriendly foreign power had attempted to impose on America, the mediocre educational performance that exists today, we might well have viewed it as an act of war. . . . We have, in effect, been committing an act of unthinking, unilateral educational disarmament. (1983, 5).

A Nation at Risk was tremendously effective as a catalyst for a flurry of school improvement initiatives throughout the United States, initiatives that came to be known as the excellence movement. Within two years of the report, more than 300 national and state task forces had investigated the condition of public schooling in America. In 41 states, legislatures mandated that students take more courses in designated academic areas. Many states raised requirements for teacher certification and tenure, and took steps to standardize curriculum, and mandated testing. The U.S. Department of Education (1984, 11) described this response to *A Nation At Risk* as "nothing short of extraordinary." Only 12 months after the Commission on Excellence had made its pronouncement on the critical state of American education, then-Secretary of Education Terrell Bell (1984, 8) reported with satisfaction that the arduous work of reform was "already bearing fruit."

This initial euphoria over the impact of the excellence movement, however, was short lived. On the fifth anniversary of its publication, the Department of Education acknowledged that the excellence initiative had failed to transform the schools (Ordovensky, 1989, A3). By the start of the new decade, the gauges on the educational indicators that had led to the publication of *A Nation at Risk* had barely moved, President Bush had announced his intention to become the "Education President," and a new report on strategies for improving American schools had been issued by the President and the nation's governors. In 1990, the United States Department of Education complained that "stagnation at relatively low levels appears to describe the level of performance of American students" (Alsalam and Ogle, 1990). As a disgruntled former official in the Department of Education wrote shortly after his resignation, "Despite all of the talk of reform, despite the investment of tons of billions of extra dollars, public education in the United States is still a failure. It is to our society what the Soviet economy is to theirs" (Finn, 1991, XIV).

By the start of the new decade, President Bush had acknowledged the failure of the excellence movement and had met with the nation's governors to identify national goals for education and strategies to achieve them. The centerpiece of this new reform strategy was the creation of "New American Schools for the Year 2000 and Beyond" (*America 2000*, 6).

What went wrong? Why had the efforts, energy, and initiatives sparked by *A Nation at Risk* proven to be so apparently ineffective? Several theories have been offered. One faults the absence of any clear goals in the excellence movement. In effect, the report of the National Commission on Excellence in Education represented merely a wringing of hands and a national exhortation for schools, teachers, and students to "do better." As Chester Finn wrote:

> School reform efforts . . . were crippled by the absence of clear objectives and the dearth of benchmarks by which progress could be gauged. . . . We were busily dashing about, sure that there was something wrong with the status quo, but uncertain quite what we wanted to accomplish instead. (1991, 28)

A second theory suggests that the failure of the excellence movement was caused by a long-standing conspiracy of the education establishment to resist any effort to change. As one school reformer concluded, "Schools are organized to maintain and defend the status quo; school systems, at least most school systems, are not organized to insure continuous improvement and development" (Schlecty, 1990, 96). Another described American schools as "classic bureaucracies, best equipped to do what they have always done" (Lezotte, 1990, 2). Chester Finn (1991, 311) is even more critical of public schools and those who work in them, describing educators as "smug, self-interested, and allergic to change," accusing them of a conspiracy to obstruct school reform, and insisting that their "fealty to the status quo" can be overcome only if the American public somehow wrests control of the schools from professional educators.

Perhaps the most widely held theory for the failure of the excellence movement is that it represented a top-down attempt to mandate improvement. While the research on effective schools and successful organizations outside of education was consistently showing the benefits of job-site autonomy and individual empowerment, the excellence movement was presented in terms of standardization and mandates. The movement was initiated and led by elected officials and business leaders and was centered in state legislatures. Practitioners were left on the outside, and the vast majority of the reform efforts were simply imposed on them. Furthermore, these reform initiatives tended toward standardization, increased reliance on rules and regulations, and detailed specifications of school practices at the expense of local school autonomy. States demonstrated an increasing willingness to trample on local prerogatives and enact laws, regulations, and mandates applicable to everyone. As one retrospective concluded, reform tactics "tended to standardize and homogenize . . . [and] inclined toward the simple, uniform, universal, and abrupt" (Finn, 1991, 42).

The failure of the top-down approach to school reform has led to what sometimes is described as the "second wave of the excellence movement." School reform efforts in the 1990's are more likely to come from local school "restructuring" than from state mandates.

"Restructuring" is to the 1990's what "excellence" was to the 1980's — a term used so widely and subjected to so many different interpretations that it lacks the specificity to be useful. Currently, almost any effort to improve a school is attributed to a commitment to restructure. However, restructuring generally is defined as "re-configuring the basic functions, operations, and organization of schools" (National LEADership Network, 1991, 1), and usually is associated with decentralization of decisions and more collegial relationships.

When the first edition of this book was written in the mid-1980's, it challenged the centralized, top-down approach to school reform and contended that the best arena for school improvement was the local school district. Thus, we regard the current attention to restructuring as a welcome event in the movement to improve schools. However, simply announcing a commitment to "restructuring" does not ensure genuinely improved conditions for teaching and learning. Altering relationships or shifting the responsibility for making decision from one group to another will not guarantee the transformation our schools require. School reform must deal not only with the rules, roles, and relationships typically addressed in restructuring, but also with the beliefs, assumptions, and values that constitute the culture of the organization. Practitioners must be willing to articulate a fundamentally new purpose of schooling. They must be willing to redefine their basic responsibilities. They must be willing to re-examine the manner in which they conduct their day-to-day business.

The *America 2000* (1991) strategy presented by President Bush is correct in asserting the need for "new American schools," schools that embrace new goals for public education and work to achieve those goals in fundamentally different ways. These schools will be created only when those within individual schools are stimulated to change the culture of their organizations and are assisted in their efforts to do so. This book attempts to offer that stimulation and assistance. It makes no attempt to resolve national education policy issues, for it is not written to or for national policy makers. It is directed to those practitioners — teachers, principals, superintendents, and Board members — who are working at the local level to improve schools one building or one district at a time. It is also aimed at the colleges and universities that seek to prepare current and future teachers and administrators to be positive change agents in the schools in which they work. It offers specific, practical recommendations on how to create an exemplary school.

In developing recommendations, we have attempted to integrate two important bodies of research that have emerged over the past decade. The first is the research on effective schools. The work of Ron Edmonds, George Weber, Michael Rutter, Wilbur Brookover, Larry Lezotte, and others has established that schools do make a difference, and that some are much more effective than others. This research has identified certain characteristics consistently found in effective schools. Many of the recommendations that we offer are based on the findings of this body of work.

The second area of research that we draw upon includes the studies of effective business practices and the leadership behind those practices. We recognize that there are important differences between the worlds of business and education. The education of a child is not equivalent to the production of an automobile. These differences should be neither ignored nor minimized. Nevertheless, we remain convinced that works such as *In Search of Excellence* by Thomas Peters and Robert Waterman (1982), *Leaders* by Warren Bennis and Burt Nanus (1985), *Reinventing the Corporation* by John Naisbitt and Patricia Aburdene (1985), *Peak Performers* by Charles Garfield (1986), *The Changemasters* by Rosabeth Moss Kanter (1983), *Corporate Cultures* by Terry Deal and Allan Kennedy (1982), *A Passion for Excellence* by Thomas Peters and Nancy Austin (1985), *The Renewal Factor* (1987) and *Adhocracy* (1990) by Robert Waterman, *Leadership is an Art* (1989) by Max DePree, *The Seven Habits of Highly Effective People* (1989) by Steven Covey, and *The Fifth Discipline* (1990) by Peter Senge are rich with ideas and information that school practitioners would do well to apply to the school setting. Unfortunately, educators have tended to overlook the important lessons that can be learned from the study of organizations outside of education.

We have attempted to overcome this tendency by merging the research on effective business practices with the research on effective schools and providing examples of how the concepts of each can be applied in the school.

This book also represents a merger of another kind, a merger of theory and practice. Too often education researchers and practitioners live in different worlds, hold different interests, and speak different languages. This book, written by a dean of a college of education whose background is in research and by a superintendent of an outstanding school district, tries to bridge the chasm between theory and practice. We have reviewed the research, but we also have interviewed school administrators from a number of nationally recognized schools to gain further insights into the actual practices that move a school toward excellence. The suggestions we offer for school improvement are both based on research and proven in practice.

The findings from the diverse sources we consulted — research on effective schools, studies of outstanding businesses, analysis of leadership, and the specific practices and procedures from a number of fine schools — were remarkably consistent. We believe they offer the framework for a systematic approach to significant school improvement. Thus, we are able to offer the following observations to those interested in moving a school toward excellence.

1) The key to school improvement is a commitment to people improvement.

A school improvement effort grounded in disdain or disregard for the professional staff is doomed to failure. It should be self-evident that the real key to improvement of any school is a commitment to the nurturing and professional development of its practitioners because, in reality, they are the school. Chapter One attempts to establish that the essential foundation of a school improvement initiative must be a recognition of the need to invest in people, support people, and develop people.

2) Excellent schools have a clear vision of what they are attempting to accomplish, what they are trying to become.

One of the most consistent findings of the research on effective organizations is that they have a vision that provides a sense of purpose, direction, and ideal future. In fact, the importance of vision has been cited so often that it has become something of a cliche. Nevertheless, schools often lack such vision. In his study for the Carnegie Foundation, Ernest Boyer (1983, 63) concluded: "High schools lack a clear and vital mission. They are unable to find common purposes or establish educational priorities that are widely shared. They seem unable to put it all together. The institution is adrift."

The essential first step in a successful school improvement initiative is developing a vision of the school's future that is locally compelling, widely understood and supported, and an accurate reflection of the personal aspirations and hopes of the individuals within the school. A school that cannot describe the ideal it seeks to become cannot create the policies to get there. Chapter Two discusses the importance of developing a widely shared vision that fosters genuine commitment rather than compliance.

3) The day-to-day operation of an excellent school is guided by a few shared central values.

Effective organizations have shared values that reflect the vision of the organization. These values help individuals to understand how they are expected to behave and serve as a mechanism for sanctioning or proscribing behavior. Furthermore, because they reflect certain parameters and standards, the values enable individuals to exercise greater autonomy, and help staff with daily decision-making. Thus, the identification, communication, and shaping of core values is a key to the success of an excellent school. Chapter Three identifies several ways in which the values of a school can be formulated and emphasized.

4) Excellent schools have principals who are effective leaders.

The importance of strong leadership has been cited again and again in both the studies of excellent businesses and the research on effective schools. But what is a strong leader—one with a vision who insists that things be done a certain way, or one who empowers others by providing them with both responsibility and autonomy? Effective principals must be able to do both. They must be forceful and aggressive promoters and protectors of the vision and values of their schools and, at the same time, provide their teachers with the freedom and autonomy to satisfy personal and professional needs. They must be strong instructional leaders and, at the same time, encourage teachers to assume more responsibility for instructional matters. They must become comfortable with a new and emerging definition of the principalship. The research on effective schools often portrays the principal in heroic terms, but the key to an improving school is not so much principals who are heroes, but principals who make heroes. Chapter Four explains that a principal need not choose between being a strong leader and empowering teachers and offers a framework for acting as both an autocratic defender of vision and values and a champion of teacher autonomy.

5) The shaping of organizational culture and climate is critical to the creation of an excellent school.

Attention to organizational culture and climate is a key factor in the success of any change effort (Sparks, 1987). The culture and climate of a school is reflected in the collective set of attitudes, beliefs, and behaviors within a building that make up the group norm (Brookover, et. al., 1979). This norm represents shared expectations for behavior and serves as a guide for what is to be done, how it is to be done, and by whom. Some of the conditions found to be present in schools that have been successful in bringing about significant improvements are: 1) a safe and orderly environment conducive to learning, 2) high expectations for both students and staff, 3) professional relationships characterized by collaboration, and 4) a willingness to experiment. Chapter Five discusses the characteristics of positive school climate and offers specific strategies for promoting those conditions in a school.

6) The curriculum of an excellent school reflects the values of the school and provides a focus that helps teachers and students "stick to the knitting."

In order to ensure a sharp focus within the organization, many successful companies operate according to the premise that "To have more than one goal is to have no goals at all." Schools, on the other hand, tend to suffer from curriculum overload. As Phillip Schlecty (1990, 69) observed, "Much of what we now do in school probably doesn't need to be done and much that should be done cannot be done so long as we keep doing what we have always done." An excellent school develops and offers a curriculum that reflects or fits the values of the school and helps to focus the attention of teachers and students on what learning is considered most significant. Chapter Six offers a process for curriculum development and suggests criteria for assessing the curriculum of a school.

7) Excellent schools monitor what is important.

Studies of effective leaders consistently conclude that these leaders communicate what the organization values by paying attention to the factors that reflect those values. An excellent school focuses on results rather than activity because a results-oriented culture is essential to school improvement. This means that procedures must be developed to enable teachers and administrators to acquire valid and useful information regarding student achievement. Furthermore, since the classroom represents the very heart of the educational enterprise, excellent schools must monitor teaching and develop procedures to promote the planning, effective instructional strategies, and reflective characteristics of good teaching. Chapter Seven provides processes for monitoring both the curriculum and teaching that are designed to both empower teachers and help schools become results-oriented enterprises.

8) In an excellent school, teachers are expected to act as leaders within their classrooms.
Teaching is multi-dimensional. Good teachers have the knowledge, strategies, and skills essential to effective instruction. Furthermore, they approach their tasks in the classroom in much the same way that effective leaders conduct themselves within their organizations. Chapter Eight provides a brief historical analysis of the role of the teacher and argues that school improvement is most likely to incur when teachers recognize that their basic responsibilities are analogous to those of the leaders of other organizations. The chapter also suggests strategies to promote this image of the teacher as leader throughout the school.

9) Excellent schools celebrate progress toward their vision and the presence of their core values with ceremonies and rituals.
Effective organizations create systems that are specifically designed to produce lots of winners and to celebrate winning it occurs. These celebrations recognize and promote the values upheld by the organization. Deal and Kennedy (1982) concluded that such ritualization and celebration of values is essential to the survival of an organization.

The celebration of values is an area that has generally been neglected by schools. Educators have been quick to advise parents of failure and slow to recognize success. Rituals and celebrations have tended to focus on athletic accomplishment or personal popularity rather than academic achievement or exemplary effort. Chapter Nine describes how schools can promote progress toward their vision as well as their core values by paying attention to celebration and ritual.

10) An excellent school is committed to continual renewal.
Robert Waterman (1987, 21) observed that "[w]ithout renewal there can be no excellence." A key to the ongoing effectiveness of any organization is its ability to renew itself — to seek and find better ways of fulfilling its mission and responding to change. However, there is a tendency in schools to accept things as they are. Perhaps the largest barrier to school improvement is the perception of the professional staff that the leadership will not sustain the initiative to see improvement through. Remembering how often they have been called on to embrace a new program only to see the interest of the district wane and the program sputter and die, teachers are likely to respond to yet

another improvement program with the ho-hum attitude of "This too shall pass."

Perhaps the single most important factor in creating an exemplary school is the willingness to pursue that goal with tenacious persistence. It is critically important that educators believe in their capacity to renew their schools. They must recognize that organizational renewal is difficult and must possess the will to continue when inevitable set-backs and temporary failures occur. An exemplary school will stay the course. Chapter Ten discusses the conditions that are associated with positive change and innovation, and it calls on those interested in school improvement to commit themselves and their schools to perpetual renewal.

There will be readers who dismiss this list of characteristics of an excellent school as idealistic. These individuals will want to know what can be done to achieve excellence in the "real world" of a particular school if its teachers are unable to agree on central values, or the principal is an ineffective leader, or procedures are not in place to monitor the curriculum.

Our response is two-fold. First, we make no apologies for offering an ideal, for it is the vision of an ideal that inspires people and organizations to make the extraordinary effort and commitment necessary to achieve excellence. Second, we believe that school improvement must be regarded as systemic change; that is, it must be viewed as a whole. To address only part of this system while ignoring other important areas reduces the likelihood that significant change will take place.

President Bush had declared that the proposal for New American Schools amounts to "nothing less than a revolution in American education" (*America 2000*, 8). However, in the final analysis, this revolution cannot be sustained by Presidential proclamations or gubernatorial education summits. The work of creating the New American Schools will fall to practitioners who will require encouragement, support, and a conceptual framework for developing significantly better conditions for teaching and learning. This book attempts to address those needs.

More than 150 years ago the English author Isaac D'Israeli observed, "It is a wretched waste to be gratified with mediocrity when the excellent lies before us." The path to excellence is available to those educators who have the determination to pursue it with tenacity. May the suggestions in this book speed their journey.

1

School Improvement Means People Improvement

*To improve [schools], one must invest
in people, support people, and develop
people.*

—Phil Schlecty
Schools for the 21st Century

The education profession was essentially a target of, rather than a participant in, the excellence movement that followed *A Nation at Risk*. The movement, initiated and lead by elected officials and business leaders and centered in state legislatures, followed a regulatory strategy that mandated uniformity among schools through heavy reliance on rules and regulations, formed top-down formal systems, and detailed specifications of school practices. Educators remained on the outside of the discussions.

The irony of this regulatory approach to improvement was that it contradicted not only the research on effective schools but also best practice in effective organizations outside of education. The research on effective schools continually found them to be reasonably autonomous and driven by the common goals and expectations of their professional staffs. Chester Finn, then Assistant Secretary of the U.S. Department of Education wrote: "The excellence movement is trying to order schools to be better; and yet, the research shows that really good schools don't respond to orders. They can grow their own" (1985, 65).

Studies of effective business practices also repeatedly cited the benefits of empowering individuals to determine their own goals and giving them the freedom to develop strategies to achieve those goals. A central message was that those closest to a given task should make the decisions as to how that task could best be completed. However, at the same time businesses and industries were initiating quality circles in the work place, the excellence movement was removing decisions from those who would ultimately be called on to carry out the school improvement initiatives.

Those who led the excellence movement disregarded several important facts. First, autonomy is an essential condition for effective teaching. The complexities of the real world of the classroom make it impossible to establish meaningful standardization of practices. As Jere Brophy and Thomas Good (1986, 370) found in their study of effective teaching:

> This research also shows that complex instructional problems cannot be solved with simple prescriptions . . . what constitutes effective instruction (even if attention is restricted to achievement as the sole outcome of interest) varies with context. What appears to be just the right amount of demandingness (or structuring of content, or praise, etc.) for one class might be too much for a second class and not enough for a third class. Even within the same class, what constitutes effective instruction will vary according to subject matter, group size, and the specific instructional objectives theme pursued.

Second, it is impossible to legislate excellence. Laws and regulations can neither substitute for nor create the common vision, shared values, and personal commitment that embody the soul of an excellent organization. If individuals work in isolation without a sense of shared purpose or common goals, an organization will not become more effective simply because it is told to do so.

Finally, the movement overlooked the obvious fact that schooling, an extremely labor-intensive endeavor, cannot be significantly improved unless practitioners are helped to enhance their effectiveness. Ernest Boyer stated the position most eloquently:

> The only way we are going to get from where we are to where we want to be is through staff development. When you talk about school improvement, you're talking about people improvement. That's the only way to improve schools unless you mean painting the buildings and fixing the floors. But that's not the school, that's the shell. The school is people, so when we talk about excellence or improvement or progress, we are really talking about the people who make up the building (Sparks, 1984, 9).

Effective organizations recognize that their greatest assets are the individuals within them, and so they make human resource development the linchpin for all improvement efforts.

In contrast, educational reform has tended to deal with the peripheral issues of schooling. New curriculum materials, alternate scheduling arrangements, different school-wide grading scales, changes in graduation requirements, or longer school days are heralded as examples of school improvement. However, genuine school improvement is not new programs and packages. Procedures and materials do not bring about change — people do.

School districts typically devote the greatest portion of their revenue to personnel, and it only makes sense that the development of this human resource must be at the very heart of a school improvement effort. Significant changes cannot occur unless there is a willingness to invest in and support teachers and principals.

Unfortunately, an extensive study of schooling practices across the nation found that programs to assist teachers and principals in professional development are generally fragmented and unfocused with no clear setting of priorities or in-depth attacks on school-wide problems (Goodlad, 1984). This haphazard approach to the development of human assets stands in marked contrast to the practice of leading business and industries. The inservice training of employees is one of the fastest growing industries in the business world today. The total corporate investment in company and business education was estimated at $40 billion each year. Harold Hodgkins calculated that the value of on-the-job training in industry approximates the net worth of the 3,500 colleges and universities in the United States (Elam, Cramer, and Brodinsky, 1986). Enlightened businesses acknowledge the benefits of ongoing training. It is time that education does the same.

BARRIERS TO CHANGE IN SCHOOLS

A variety of theories have been offered as to why schools are so slow to accept change. One (Carlson, 1965) suggests that because they do not confront the competitive pressures, schools have become accustomed to a guaranteed existence and thus have lost the incentive to change, which arises out of the struggle for survival. The monopoly enjoyed by public schools has led school practitioners to become "sluggish," "inefficient," "smug," and "allergic to change" in the eyes of some critics (Finn, 1991, 90). The call for "school choice" and "competition among schools" is grounded, in part, on this theory.

Another barrier to change that has been cited is a weak knowledge base. Carlson (1965, 5) wrote: "It is rare indeed when an educational innovation is backed by solid research. It is even rarer to find an educational innovation which has been fully developed and subjected to careful trial and experimentation." In agriculture a prototypical farm is established to persuade farmers of the benefits of new methods and materials. Changes in medical practice are preceded by experimentation and verification. Schools, on the other hand, do not feel obligated to change because there are no models that offer compelling evidence of a new and better way of conducting the business of schooling.

A third barrier to change is that Americans disagree about the goals of education, and thus schools have no clear mandate as to which innovations to pursue. In fact, any proposal to change school practices in a truly significant way is likely to be met with skepticism from parents who have a view of schooling anchored in their own experience. Proposals to change educational practices are likely to elicit a response of "that's not how it was when I was in school, and I turned out okay." While there is widespread concern regarding the general state of education in this country, parents tend to look favorably on their local schools. As a result, practitioners have little incentive to change when reform efforts are likely to meet with local resistance.

Another explanation for the difficulties schools have in attempting to change is that they typically are organized in a way that discourages people from considering problems from a broad perspective. All too frequently schools are characterized by rigid departmental or grade-level structures, adversarial relationships between teachers and administrators, territorial disputes among staff members, and the inability of individuals to see the larger picture. Purkey and Smith (1983) described schools as loosely-coupled systems in which classrooms are isolated workplaces subject to little organizational control. One elementary school principal was less generous, describing his faculty as "twenty-four different people in twenty-four different rooms united by a common parking lot." Schools must escape from this segmentalist thinking if they are ever to become receptive to significant change.

Organizations that are resistant to change are prone to what Kanter (1983) has described as "segmentalist thinking." In these organizations problems are viewed as narrowly as possible, independent of their context, and independent of their connections to other problems. Kanter (1983, 33) wrote: "Companies with segmentalist cultures are likely to have segmentalist structures: a large number of compartments walled off from one another—department from department, level above from level below, field office from headquarters, labor from management, or men from women." The result is that individual employees often focus on their personal tasks rather than the greater purpose of the enterprise. Senge (1990, 19) referred to this tendency as an "organizational learning disability" and argued that "when people in organizations focus only on their positions, they have little responsibility for the results produced when all positions interact." Unfortunately, the description of the segmentalist culture aptly depicts many school districts.

Yet another factor that interferes with school change is the lack of self-efficacy that characterizes some teachers and administrators. If the faculty and administration believe that the causes of learning lie outside their sphere of influence — in the genes or the socioeconomic status of their students — they will not be motivated to improve their effectiveness. Often this pessimism is expressed in the assertion that schools cannot improve until society addresses its larger problems of poverty, homelessness, negligent and abusive parents, too much television, etc. Once this reasoning is accepted, schools are no longer responsible for improving; in fact, attempts to initiate reform will seem fruitless or ridiculous.

Finally, perhaps the biggest reason that schools are resistant to change is simply because the people within them, like all human beings, seek a state of equilibrium. Change suggests at least temporary disequilibrium and discomfort and thus is viewed as something to be avoided. Those who hope to initiate a school improvement program must recognize that concern and anxiety are inevitable by-products of asking people to change, and they must develop a systematic plan to overcome those reactions.

HELPING PRACTITIONERS COPE WITH CHANGE

The Concerns-Based Adoption Model (CBAM) of staff development (Hord, et al., 1987) has attempted to identify the stages of concern that teachers are likely to experience as they learn about, prepare for, and use a new practice. The stages of concern typically flow from a focus on self, to managerial issues associated with the task, to the impact of the program. In the early stages, teachers seek information on the innovation—how it is similar to and different from what they are already doing, the nature and extent of the training they are to receive, how they will benefit from that training, etc. As final preparations are made for the teachers to begin using the innovation, task concerns dealing with time become more intense. In the third phase of concerns, teachers address the effects of the innovation upon their students and consider what can be done to improve the effectiveness of the program. If an effort is made to identify and address these concerns as they emerge, the potential for the ultimate success of the program is increased. Hord and her colleagues (1987) offered the following suggestions for interventions at the various levels of concern:

Stage 0: Awareness Concerns
("What is the innovation?")

- If possible, involve teachers in discussions and decisions about the innovation and its implementation.
- Share enough information to arouse interest, but not so much that it overwhelms.
- Acknowledge that a lack of awareness is expected and reasonable, and that no questions about the innovation are foolish.
- Encourage unaware persons to talk with colleagues who know about the innovation.

- Take steps to minimize gossip and inaccurate sharing of information about the innovation.

Stage 1: Information Concerns
("I need to know more about the innovation.")

- Provide clear and accurate information about the innovation.
- Use a variety of ways to share information — verbally, in writing, and through any available media. Communicate with individuals and with small and large groups.
- Have persons who have used the innovation in other settings visit with your teachers. Visits to user schools could also be arranged.
- Help teachers see how the innovation relates to their current practices, both in regard to similarities and differences.
- Be enthusiastic and enhance the visibility of others who are excited.

Stage 2: Personal Concerns
("How will the innovation affect me?")

- Legitimize the existence and expression of personal concerns. Knowing that these concerns are common and that others have them can be comforting.
- Use personal notes and conversations to provide encouragement and reinforce personal adequacy.
- Connect these teachers with others whose personal concerns have diminished and who will be supportive.
- Show how the innovation can be implemented sequentially rather than in one big leap. It is important to establish expectations that are attainable.
- Do not push innovation use, but encourage and support it while maintaining expectations.

Stage 3: Management Concerns
("How will I find time to do this?")

- Clarify the steps and components of the innovation.
- Provide answers that address the small, specific "how-to" issues that are so often the cause of management concerns.
- Demonstrate exact and practical solutions to the logistical problems that contribute to these concerns.
- Help teachers sequence specific activities and set timelines for their accomplishments.

- Attend to the immediate demands of the innovation, not what will be or could be in the future.

Stage 4: Consequence Concerns
("How is my use of the innovation affecting kids?")

- Provide these individuals with opportunities to visit other settings in which the innovation is in use and to attend conferences on the topic.
- Provide them with positive feedback and needed support.
- Find opportunities for these staff members to share their skills with others.
- Share information pertaining to the innovation with them.

Stage 5: Collaboration
("I would like to discuss my findings and ideas with others.")

- Provide these individuals with opportunities to develop those skills necessary for working collaboratively.
- Bring together those persons, both within and outside the school, who are interested in collaboration.
- Help the collaborators establish reasonable expectations and guidelines for the collaborative effort.
- Use them to provide technical assistance to others who need assistance.
- Encourage the collaborators, but do not attempt to force collaboration on those who are not interested.

Stage 6: Refocusing Concerns
("I have an idea for improving upon the innovation.")

- Respect and encourage the interest that these persons have for finding a better way.
- Help channel their ideas and energies in ways that will be productive rather than counterproductive.
- Encourage them to act on their concerns for program improvement.
- Help them access the resources they may need to refine their ideas and put them into practice.
- Be aware of and willing to accept the fact that these staff members may replace or significantly modify the existing innovations.

One of the most effective means of resolving teacher concerns is simply to provide a structure that promotes dialogue among teachers (Lieberman and Miller, 1981; Sparks, 1987). There is growing evidence that creating small, supportive groups in which teachers are encouraged to discuss their questions, concerns, and ideas about a new program enhances the eventual adoption of the program. Groups should be kept to eight or fewer participants in order to encourage discussion and should have the benefit of a facilitator to help keep the group focused on solutions. Having the opportunity to discuss problems they may be encountering helps reduce the isolation that teachers often feel in initiating a new program. Furthermore, the small-group format provides a forum for the sharing of successes and testimonials needed to fuel the improvement effort. In short, giving teachers the opportunity to discuss the improvement program is a critically significant aspect of staff development and teacher growth.

Robert Eaker and Jim Huffman (1980) developed a consumer-validation approach to assisting teachers with change that uses the small-group format and recognizes that teachers will need to test an innovation in their own classrooms before they will embrace it fully. This approach is based on the assumption that before teachers will be willing to become "consumers" of research, they must first act as "testers" to determine the effects of implementing the findings in their classroom. The consumer-validation procedure includes three steps:

1. *Research reporting seminars.* The primary purpose of these seminars is to provide teachers with a clear understanding of research findings on a particular topic such as time on task, questioning strategies, or classroom management. The findings are synthesized and presented as clearly and concisely as possible. Teachers are then invited to brainstorm specific activities or strategies for implementing the research findings in their classrooms.

2. *Classroom implementation.* During the next three to four weeks, teachers apply the research by initiating some of the strategies or activities that were identified in the brainstorming sessions. Then teachers are asked to reflect on and evaluate the results of their efforts. Forms are provided to enable teachers to briefly describe the activities and strategies they attempted and their reactions to what occurred.

3. *Sharing sessions.* In this final stage, the seminar groups reconvene and teachers share their findings. These sessions serve two important purposes. First, the pooling of information gives teachers new ideas to try in their own classrooms. The "testimonial" of a colleague is of tremendous value in motivating teachers to pursue an idea. Teachers tend to hold the experiences of a colleague in much higher regard than the findings of a researcher. Second, the sessions give teachers an opportunity to interact with each other about

teaching. Unfortunately, teaching is rarely the subject of meetings that teachers are asked to attend. Simply increasing the dialogue among teachers on the topic of teaching can have a positive effect on a faculty's sense of professionalism.

The recognition that teachers need an opportunity to try out proposals for change is also a key feature of a model of staff development offered by Bruce Joyce and Beverly Showers (1983). They proposed that the following elements be included in training programs to assist teachers who are attempting to change.

1. *Recognition of the difficulty of transfer.* It is difficult to transfer new information or new skills into everyday practice. Even though a new skill has been explained and demonstrated, staff members are likely to need practice and coaching before they are actually able to include the skill in their repertoire.

2. *A high degree of skill development.* It is simply not reasonable to expect that poorly developed skills will be transferred. Thorough training conducted over an adequate amount of time is essential for effective staff development.

3. *Development of executive control.* Teachers must have the intellectual "scaffolding" necessary not only to perform a skill, but also to judge when its use is appropriate. As Joyce and Showers (1983, 22) noted, "Not until a teacher can select the strategy when it is appropriate to do so, modifying it to fit the characteristics of the student, implement it, and assess its effectiveness can we say he or she has achieved an adequate degree of executive control."

4. *Practice in the workplace.* One of the most consistent and emphatic messages of the research on teacher change is that teachers need sustained practice in the classroom with frequent feedback in order to gain mastery of a new skill or strategy. In fact, some research suggests that teachers must use a new skill twenty to thirty times before they have sufficient mastery to incorporate it in their teaching repertoire, use it comfortably, and adapt it to the needs of their students (Showers, Joyce, and Bennett, 1987).

5. *Coaching.* Teachers often need ongoing feedback and support from someone who has mastered the skills that they are trying to learn. In fact, the bad news is that without the benefit of coaching from either supervisors or peers, teachers are unlikely to sustain practice until they have gained mastery of a new skill regardless of their initial enthusiasm. The good news is that with coaching, "nearly all teachers...[are able] to sustain practice and gain executive control over a large range of curricular and instructional practices" (Joyce, Show-

ers, and Bennett, 1987,86). Some of the benefits of coaching include:

a. *The provision of companionship.* By providing for interaction with another human being, coaching gives teachers the support they need to tackle a difficult process.

b. *The provision for technical feedback.* Coaching provides teachers with feedback as they practice new models of teaching.

c. *The analysis of application.* Coaching helps teachers analyze what they might accomplish by making further adjustments.

d. *Adaptation to students.* Coaching helps teachers "read" the responses of their students. Teachers need to be able to read responses correctly in order to decide whether they need further training in how they might adapt the particular skill they are practicing.

e. *Promotion of the ability to "learn how to learn."* Coaching promotes a learning aptitude that empowers teachers to learn in new situations and to solve problems as they arise.

PROMOTING A COMMITMENT TO CHANGE

There are certainly a great many barriers to bringing about change in school, and those who seek to do so must be realistic enough to recognize the difficulty of the task. However, if teachers and administrators can be helped to believe in their capacity to bring about change, if their issues and concerns are addressed, and if a sustained level of appropriate support can be provided, these barriers can be overcome. The challenge is to identify and create conditions that promote the professional commitment to bring about meaningful change. One recent study (Rosenholtz and Simpson, 1990) found the following factors influential in generating teacher commitment.

1. *Performance efficacy.* A primary factor in teacher commitment is the sense that one does matter, that it is possible to solve the challenges.

2. *Psychic rewards.* Teachers accrue psychic dividends from external recognition by valued colleagues. The absence of feedback, especially about the positive results of one's efforts, tends to figure largely in teacher dissatisfaction.

3. *Task autonomy and discretion.* The extent to which the work provides substantial freedom and discretion to carry out tasks is a valued part of the teacher's work.

4. *Learning opportunities.* School settings that facilitate learning opportunities, foster exchanges of ideas, and introduce new ideas may increase teachers' commitment by expanding the meaningfulness and

professional stature of the work. The absence of opportunities for professional growth has been found to be related to the dissatisfaction of teachers.

5. *School management of students' behavior.* The way the school manages the behavior of students is an organizational resource that affects how much time teachers are able to devote to the core tasks of instruction.

6. *Buffering by the principal.* The ability of a teacher to teach is heavily influenced by the extent to which the principal is able to protect the teacher from a variety of non-teaching tasks that interfere with instructional routine.

A study by the Rand Corporation (McLaughlin, 1990) of change efforts in schools across the nation reinforced the belief that the best hope for school reform lies in improving schools one building at a time. Among the organizational factors that were found to support improvement efforts were collegial relationships, organizational structures that promote open communication and feedback, and leadership that promotes opportunities for professional growth.

STRATEGIES FOR BASING SCHOOL IMPROVEMENT UPON PEOPLE IMPROVEMENT

The key to school improvement is people improvement. Attention to professional development must be the cornerstone of any initiative to enhance the effectiveness of schools. The following strategies are recommended to ensure proper attention to this critical aspect of school improvement.

1. Review the efforts and resources devoted to the professional development of staff in the past year. List the efforts made to develop the human resources in your school.

2. Develop a list of ideas for enhancing the efforts of your school to develop its human resources.

3. Meet in small groups to assess the barriers to change in your school. Attempt to reach consensus as to the degree those barriers are present in your school.

4. Discuss an innovation that was attempted in your school without success. Identify the factors that led to its demise and speculate as to what might have been done to ensure its success.

5. Create a consumer-validation group to identify and implement a classroom innovation.

6. Develop a proposal to use peer coaching frequently in your school.

7. Ask teachers to rank your school on a scale from one (low) to five (high) in each of the six areas of organizational climate related to teacher commitment. Establish teacher task forces to address areas rated as low.

2

Developing a Shared Vision of an Excellent School

If there is a spark of genius in the
leadership function at all it must be in
this transcending ability, a kind of
magic, to assemble—out of all the
variety of images, signals, forecasts
and alternatives—a clearly articulated
vision of the future that is at once
single, easily understood, clearly
desirable, and energizing.

—Warren Bennis and Burt Nanus,
Leaders

Building shared vision must be seen as
a central element of the daily work of
leaders. It is ongoing and never-ending.

—Peter Senge,
The Fifth Discipline

Effective organizations have a shared sense of purpose, a direction, or what the literature on organizational effectiveness commonly refers to as a "shared vision." Schools can be (and in many instances are) organizations with an overriding purpose and a sense of shared commitment. Such schools have a sense of identity and a shared view of the future, essential prerequisites for a healthy organization. Shared vision provides the blueprint for a school improvement program, and thus the effort to improve a school must start with a process to arrive at this shared vision.

DESCRIBING THE SCHOOL YOU SEEK TO BECOME

Sincere people in various roles in the school community genuinely endorsed the goal of excellence for their schools. After all, who can be anti-excellence? But, the fact that disparate groups might endorse the general concept of an excellent school does not provide a district with either a meaningful consensus or a clearly defined goal. Various board members, veteran teachers, school administrators, and students probably all have their own concepts of an excellent school. A district is not provided with a useful self-image if it makes no attempt to move the concept of an excellent school from the general to the specific. A goal as vague as achieving excellence fails to give direction or purpose. The vision of the school that is to be created must be fairly specific. Simply put, school practitioners who are unable to describe what an ideal school would look like will be unable to develop the policies to create an ideal school. The wisdom of the adage applies here: If you don't know where you are going you probably aren't going to get there.

The critical importance of vision has been cited by those who have studied effective businesses and effective leaders. John Naisbitt and Patricia Aburdene (1985, 24) concluded that the first ingredient in establishing an outstanding company is a "powerful vision, a whole new sense of where a company is going and how to get there." In their highly regarded study of leadership, Warren Bennis and Burt Nanus (1985, 89) explained that vision "articulates a view of a realistic, credible, attractive future for the organization, a condition that is better in some important ways than what now exists. A vision is a target that beckons." Thus it is shared vision that provides an organization with a sense of purpose, direction, and ideal future state.

Several benefits accrue to the district that describes the school it wishes to provide. The first is in the subtle but significant area of attitude. Excellence in any field is unattainable unless someone has the will, the desire, or the passion to achieve great things. This process results in a public pronouncement that a particular district is committed to the lofty goal of working toward an ideal. There is a heightened awareness of that goal on the part of the various publics that constitute a district, and those who embrace the goal have a focal point around which to rally. When people have a vision, they are motivated to make it a reality.

A second major benefit is the direction it gives to individuals within the organization. If an organization has a clear sense of its purpose, direction, and ideal future state, its members are able to find and understand their roles within that organization. Diverse activities are given coherence when they are placed in the context of a common vision. Very clear guidelines for individual conduct and decisions begin to emerge. These guidelines can be explicitly enumerated to provide a concise statement of the core values or principles that each individual will be expected to observe.

A third benefit of describing the ideal school is that it helps a school establish an agenda for action. Once a description exists, current policies, practices, and conditions can be evaluated to identify any discrepancies between the reality of the existing school and the characteristics of the ideal school. If a school has no idea where it is going, the clarity and focus on what needs to be done is impossible to obtain.

USING RESEARCH AS A BASIS FOR DEVELOPING A FRAMEWORK FOR EXCELLENCE

It is important to recognize the contribution research can play in describing an excellent school. Research findings can provide a frame of reference for thinking about characteristics consistently associated with effective schooling. These findings should be viewed not as a simple recipe for reform, but rather as a theoretical framework around which a plan for school improvement can be developed.

The School Effectiveness Research

Ideas about excellence—particularly excellence in schooling—change periodically. Traditionally, measures of excellence in schooling have emphasized such factors as college degrees earned by the faculty, class size, the number of library books, and the adequacy of the facility. These aspects of schooling still form the basic criteria for most school accreditation programs.

Periodically in the history of education, the effectiveness of schooling has been equated with the degree to which students were prepared to enter the world of work. This emphasis has usually surfaced during periods of high unemployment or recession. During such times, the focus has been on vocational education, career education, and career counseling.

During the late 1960s and the 1970s, the prevailing attitude within the research community was that, by and large, schools made very little difference in student achievement. The Coleman Report, Racial Isolation in the Public Schools, and Disequality were among the studies which argued that the socioeconomic status of a child's family was responsible, more than any other factor, for student achievement. This led to the conclusion among some educators that because schools could not do very much to affect student achievement, an excellent school was one that created an atmosphere where kids enjoyed school and learned to feel good about themselves.

In 1979 Michael Rutter and others published results that directly challenged the assumption that schools make very little difference in student achievement. Although a few studies conducted as early as 1974 had examined schooling practices and academic achievement, Rutter's *Fifteen Thousand Hours* (1979) brought this issue to the forefront. Additional studies by Brookover and Lezotte (1979) and Phi Delta Kappa

(1980) supported Rutter's findings. The research of Ron Edmonds (1979) on school effectiveness may have contributed more than any other study to the widespread recognition that what schools do, does affect the achievement of students. The following characteristics were consistently found in effective schools:

1. safe and orderly environment
2. clear and focused school mission
3. instructional leadership
4. high expectations
5. opportunity to learn and high time on task
6. frequent monitoring of student progress
7. positive home-school relations

The Northwest Regional Educational Laboratory (1990) provides a useful synthesis of the research on effective schools. This synthesis, focusing on studies that identified schooling practices and characteristics associated with measurable improvements in student achievement and behavior, provides the following picture of an effective school:

1. Everyone emphasizes the importance of learning.
2. The curriculum is based on clear goals and objectives.
3. Students are grouped to promote effective instruction.
4. School time is used for learning.
5. Discipline is firm and consistent.
6. There are pleasant conditions for teaching and learning.
7. Strong leadership guides the instructional program.
8. Teachers and administrators continually strive to improve instructional effectiveness.
9. Staff engage in ongoing professional development and collegial learning activities.
10. There are high expectations for quality instruction.
11. Incentives and rewards are used to build strong student and staff motivation.
12. Parents and community members are invited to become involved.
13. Learning progress is monitored closely.
14. Students at risk of school failure are provided programs to help them succeed.

Stewart Purkey and Marshall Smith (1983) conducted a review of the research on school effectiveness and identified what they believe are the most important characteristics of effective schools. Purkey and Smith grouped characteristics into two categories: 1) organizational and structural variables, and 2) process-form variables. The organizational and structural variables include:

- school site management
- leadership
- staff stability
- curriculum articulation and organization
- staff development
- parental involvement and support
- school-wide recognition of academic success
- maximized learning time
- district support

The process-form variables associated with school effectiveness are:

- collaborative planning and collegial relationships
- sense of community
- clear goals and high expectations that are commonly shared
- order and discipline

Researchers may disagree about a particular finding or a particular research methodology, but research on effective schools does provide a surprisingly clear and consistent picture of school practices and characteristics associated with student achievement. Thus, although the findings are not a recipe for quick success, they do form a useful framework for thinking about and planning for school improvement.

Research from America's Best-Run Companies

Another valuable resource in the research base that should underlie a school improvement initiative is found in the studies of organizations outside of education. Research findings on such topics as organizational climate, organizational effectiveness, personnel development, leadership, and organizational change provide a portrait of a healthy, vital organization and are often applicable to schools.

One of the most widely read descriptions of common characteristics of excellent companies is *In Search of Excellence* (1982) by Thomas Peters and Robert Waterman. This study of the factors that have contributed to the success of America's best-run companies is rich with information on leadership and organizational climate that can be applied readily to schools. The ideas in this book and others like it should be made available to those attempting to describe an excellent school. These ideas can serve as an effective catalyst for discussions of those characteristics other than academic achievement that are important ingredients of excellence. A brief summary of the conclusions reached by Peters and Waterman is presented below. Specific applications of their findings to the school setting will be discussed throughout this book.

1. *The best-run companies show a bias for action, for getting things done.* Excellent companies get quick action because their organizations are fluid. "These companies are characterized by a vast network of informal, open communications...The right people get into contact with each other regularly....[There is] a virtual technology of keeping in touch" (1982, 121-23).

2. *The best companies stick close to the customer.* Excellent companies learn from the people they serve. These companies are good listeners and get many of their best ideas from their customers.

3. *Excellent companies encourage autonomy and entrepreneurship.* Outstanding companies foster many leaders and innovators throughout the organization. Managers in these companies do not launch a new project unless an individual zealot or champion volunteers to embrace that project and becomes personally committed to its success.

4. *The best-run companies achieve productivity through people.* Managers in excellent companies realize that a prime motivational factor is the individual's perception that he or she is doing well. Consequently, these companies set goals that most people can reach and let employees know when they are doing well. These firms celebrate success with ceremony and hoopla.

5. *The best companies are hands-on, value-driven organizations.* In excellent companies, top management stays close to the action —walking plant floors, visiting stores, and so on. These leaders believe in "management by wandering about." And they continually remind employees of the organization's values and mission.

6. *Excellent companies stick to their knitting.* The best-run companies stay with the basics rather than diversifying their goals or tasks.

7. *The best-run companies maintain a simple form and a lean staff.* The best-run corporations have a structure that is "elegantly simple." Top-level staffs are lean.

8. *Excellent companies are simultaneously "loose" and "tight."* Even as they encourage individual initiative and autonomy ("looseness"), the best companies also demand rigid adherence ("tightness") to a few core values that drive and give direction to everyone in the organization.

There are many other books that are particularly helpful in developing strategies for school improvement. Peter Senge's *The Fifth Discipline* (1990) makes a compelling case for the importance of developing a shared vision. *On Leadership* (1990) by John Gardner provides valuable insight into leadership behavior in successful organizations. *Thriving on Chaos* (1987) by Tom Peters is a virtual handbook on organizational visioning and values. The point is, a great deal is known about successful organizations—what they look like and how they act—and while no book should be regarded as a recipe for school improvement, leaders of school improvement initiatives should become students of organizational behavior and leadership.

REACHING CONSENSUS ON VISION

The ultimate value of a school's definition or vision of excellence will depend not on its format but on whether it elicits feelings of ownership and endorsement from the various groups in the school district. School leaders who feel certain of the direction they want their schools to take and who are impatient to initiate school improvement may be tempted to draft a personal vision statement for their schools and present it as a *fait accompli*. That temptation should be resisted. If an organization is to be successful, it must be guided by a vision that has grown from the needs of the entire organization and is claimed or owned by all important actors. As Senge (1990, 214) concluded, "The origin of a vision is less important than the process whereby it comes to be shared. It isn't truly a shared vision until it connects with the personal visions of those within the organization."

Those who hope to lead school improvement efforts must recognize that vision cannot be established by edict or coercion. They must understand that the involvement of appropriate people in a consensus decision-making process will have an important influence on the degree of commitment to sustaining an improvement effort in the school. Involvement leads to the feeling that the definition of excellence is one's own. Too often teachers are asked to commit themselves to someone else's notions about what they should value. If teachers, administrators, and parents are to be genuinely committed to achieving an excellent school, they must play an important part in reaching a consensus about the school they seek to provide.

Involving a variety of people in a consensus decision-making process is difficult, time-consuming, and often frustrating. Disagreements will arise, time will be wasted, and there will be moments when things seem to come to a standstill. At such times, school leaders must provide the direction necessary to maintain the group cohesiveness and move the process along. They must realize that it is much better to resolve controversial issues during this early stage of the school improvement process than to wait and have them coming up repeatedly during the day-to-day operation of the school.

Developing a Vision Statement

One way to address the issue of reaching a consensus on a compelling vision of the future of a school is to establish a task force for that purpose. The composition of this task force and its ability to achieve consensus can be the major factors in determining the general support for a school improvement effort. Thus the question of who will serve on the committee is an important one. It is a mistake to simply invite volunteers; membership on the committee is much too important to be left to chance. Those initiating the school improvement effort should identify key individuals to be invited to serve on the committee. The following factors should be taken into consideration:

1. *The diverse groups within the school district should be represented.* The committee should include representatives of the major groups that form a school community—teachers, parents, administrators, students, community members, business leaders, etc. Since the main responsibility for implementing a school improvement plan will generally fall on teachers, they should be heavily represented on the committee.

2. *The individuals chosen should be influential within the groups they represent.* Every faculty, every student body, and every community includes highly regarded individuals who are able to influence opinion within their group. These key actors should be identified and encouraged to participate on the committee.

3. *Committee members must be able to maintain a broad perspective.* Members of the committee must have the capacity to examine ideas and proposals in terms of their total impact on the school. They also must be able to consider and appreciate different points of view. The committee is no place for single-issue zealots who are unwilling to compromise.

4. *Key policy makers must be included.* Nothing will extinguish enthusiasm for the effort to create an excellent school more quickly than the refusal of policy makers to enact the proposals of the committee after it has arrived at a consensus. Therefore, it is highly advisable to include one of the key decision makers of the school on this committee. A superintendent, principal, or influential member of the board of education can caution the committee if it begins to exceed the parameters of its mission and can help win final approval for recommendations.

5. *The principal should chair the committee.* Since working with groups in reaching consensus is a very difficult and time-consuming task, principals may tend to turn this job over to someone else— perhaps a supervisor, a consultant, or a professor from a nearby university. Al-

though this approach may be less trying, it has some very real problems that will manifest themselves in the long run. The principal must model the importance of school improvement by making a personal commitment to the process.

Although the principal should lead the group's effort to improve the school, his or her leadership style should ensure teamwork, collaboration, and group decision-making. Thus, the principal must be skilled in group processes and consensus building. The success of the task force will depend to a great degree on the interpersonal and communications skills of the principal. If the committee resorts to simple majority rule to arrive at decisions, there will inevitably be winners and losers on every issue. This, in turn, will make it more difficult to win broad support for the final product of the committee. It is unlikely that each member of the group will support every decision as the very best available option. Nevertheless, it is the responsibility of the principal to keep an issue before the group until it has reached a decision that all members agree to support.

At the initial meeting of the committee, the principal should help the group define its purpose. Subsequent misunderstandings and misdirected efforts are less likely if the committee agrees to a succinct statement of purpose at the outset. Some advocates of the consensus process argue that this statement of purpose should emerge from the initial discussions of the committee. However, the purpose or charge of the committee should already have been defined, at least in general terms, by the school district. Therefore, the leader can expedite the work of the committee if he or she presents a tentative statement of purpose as a basis for discussion. The leader then can demonstrate the consensus process for decision making as the group considers this statement.

Once the group has agreed to a statement of purpose and understands the consensus-building process that it will try to follow in making decisions, the leader should present the group with a concise summary of the key findings of the research on effective schools. Once again, this research has been remarkably consistent in identifying the characteristics of effective schools, and members of the committee should have the benefit of its findings. This brief review of research, presented in nontechnical terms, also will ensure some common background information for members.

Next, the committee must decide how it will proceed with its task. One effective strategy for developing a consensus is simply to ask a number of different groups to respond to one or more of these key questions:

1. What do you believe are the characteristics of an exemplary school?

2. In what ways would you like our school to be significantly different three years from now?

3. What have we accomplished in the past three years that you find as a source of pride?

4. What can we do in the next three years that would make us proud?

The leader should remind the committee that general support for its final recommendations is best fostered by engaging the different segments of the school community in discussion of the type of school they would like to have in that community. The ultimate goal of the committee should be to arrive at a description of an excellent school that teachers, parents, students, and community members will endorse.

Members of the task force then are assigned to meet with various constituencies—teachers, parents, students, business representatives, etc.—to conduct discussions of these questions. Simple brainstorming techniques are generally quite effective in this phase of the process. Each individual participating in the discussion is invited to generate responses, which are recorded on a chalkboard. At this point, no comments about the relative merit of the ideas are allowed. When all the ideas have been listed on the board, similar responses are consolidated. After the consolidated list has been generated, the participants discuss the merits of each characteristic. Each member then ranks the items in the list from the most essential to the least essential. Voting should not be allowed. Rather, the group should continue its discussion until it has reached a consensus that each member of the group can support.

Each member of the task force presents his or her findings to the full task force in the form of a list of desired characteristics, goals, or achievements. As each report is presented, the group looks for common themes or trends in the responses. Once these themes have been identified, the first draft of the findings of the task force is developed. This step normally is carried out between meetings. The draft statement then is presented to different constituencies for feedback, and is refined at subsequent meetings until it is acceptable to the entire group. Once the task force has completed its final draft and won the approval of the board of education for its description of an excellent school, the major work of the task force is finished.

This process can be adapted to fit various situations. It can be simplified for smaller groups. Successful use of the technique with larger, more heterogeneous groups will require more work and planning. But regardless of the complexity of the process, the essential idea is this: reaching a consensus on what the school seeks to become is the critical first step in improving a school. The format of the finished product is not a significant issue. Whether it results in a short list or a long narrative is less important than the fact that the groups involved have achieved consensus on the final products. An example of some areas to consider in developing this consensus is found in the appendix.

Several cautions are in order for those about to undertake the development of a written vision statement for a school. The first caveat regards the process. Because of the increasing recognition of the importance of vision statements, writing them has become something of a fad. Many school administrators have been presented mandates to "write a vision," and they often respond by looking for a simple recipe to make the task as painless as possible. As Tom Peters (1987,486) wrote, "the idea of developing a vision statement is too important to be trivialized by the explosion of handbooks on ' how to get a vision' in twenty-seven easy steps." Developing a shared vision may take time; but if the goal is significant school improvement, it is time well spent.

The second caution deals with the product of the vision statement. There is a tendency to write broad, generic statements that are abstractly unassailable but completely useless in terms of giving direction to individual teachers. "We will release the human potential in every child so that each will be able to function effectively in the highly technological, multi-cultural society of the twenty-first century" and similar statements may sound terrific, but they serve no useful purpose. Vision statements should be specific enough that school personnel can determine what they need to do to make the vision become a reality. Jargon-filled tomes should not be confused with effective vision statements.

EVALUATING A VISION STATEMENT

On what basis should a vision statement be evaluated? The following questions provide useful criteria.

1. *Is it written?* School leaders who delude themselves if they believe that those within their organization recognize and understand the desired future state of the school despite the fact that no one has taken the trouble to describe it in writing. People do not acquire this understanding through osmosis. The process of writing a statement helps to sharpen issues and clarify positions. Although putting a vision statement in writing does not ensure that it will be effective in influencing individuals within the organization, the lack of a written statement suggests inattention to this important aspect of organizational life.

2. *Is it widely disseminated?* If a vision statement is to influence the decisions and behavior of those within the organization, they must be aware of it. The statement should appear in faculty manuals, parent handbooks, student guidebooks, and any other school publication with a

wide dissemination. An effort should constantly be made to call attention to the statement.

3. *Is it widely supported?* The effect of the vision statement will be directly correlated to the level of support that it has within the school community. Once again, it must reflect the hopes, aspirations, and personal visions of those who are called on to make it a reality.

4. *Is it used in the day-to-day operation?* An effective vision statement serves as a blueprint for school improvement. It simply cannot be filed away and forgotten. It should serve as a constant reference point, a guiding star in the establishment of goals, programs, procedures, and priorities. Effective organizations are not characterized by high-sounding vision statements floating in space, but rather by a relentless willingness to examine current conditions in light of an explicitly stated desired future. A shared vision is not brought about by the drafting of a statement. It can become a reality only as a direct result of the efforts of committed individuals who make the advancement of that vision central to their daily work.

STRATEGIES FOR DEVELOPING A STATEMENT OF EXCELLENCE

Excellent organizations are characterized by a common understanding about where the organization is headed and about what is valued. Schools are no exception. If schools are to improve significantly, they must first develop a sense of what they want to become. Following are strategies recommended to school leaders interested in developing a shared vision statement.

1. Gain the approval of the board of education for initiating a process to develop a vision statement for your school.

2. Create a task force to oversee the process and invite key individuals to serve on the task force. Selection should take into account representation of the diverse groups within the school district, the influence of the individual within his or her group, and the ability of the person to take a broad view when considering the ramifications of school improvement efforts. A key policy maker in the district also should be included on the committee. It should be led by the principal.

3. Ask the board to develop an explicit, written charge to the task force.

4. Convene an initial meeting of the task force at which group members should become acquainted with the consensus process for decision making, agree on a statement of purpose, review the

parameters of their responsibility, and become familiar with the research on effective schools and their practices.

5. Assign to members of the task force the responsibility to survey different segments of the school community on one or more of the following questions: What are the characteristics of an excellent school? What would we like our school to look like three years from now? What has our school accomplished in the past three years that makes us proud? and What can we accomplish in the next three years to make us proud? The survey should include parents, teachers, business representatives, and community members. Students should be included at the upper grade levels.

6. Arrange a series of neighborhood coffees and small group meetings to discuss these questions.

7. Arrange to be placed on the agenda of local businesses and service groups to discuss these questions with their members.

8. Faithfully record the ideas presented during each discussion.

9. Ask each member of the task force to report his or her findings to the group.

10. Analyze the specifics of each report and identify the most prevalent themes in the responses.

11. When the group has reached consensus on the most prevalent themes identified in the survey, assign an individual or subcommittee to develop a first draft of the vision statement that is based on the findings of the task force.

12. After the task force has reviewed the initial draft, submit it to representatives of various constituencies for reaction and feedback.

13. Revise as needed until consensus has been reached on the task force.

14. Present the recommended vision statement to the board of education for consideration and ask that it be adopted as board policy or the approved district practice.

15. Invite various constituencies (teachers, parents, business representatives, etc.) to identify discrepancies between the ideal described in the vision statement and the existing conditions in the school.

3

Shared Values: The Essence of Excellence

*...[I]t is clear that organizations have,
in fact, gained great strength from
shared values — with emphasis on
"shared." If employees know what
their company stands for, if they know
what standards to uphold, then they
are much more likely to make decisions
that support those standards. They are
also more likely to feel as if they are an
important part of the organization.
They are motivated because life in the
company has meaning for them.*

—Terry E. Deal and Allan A. Kennedy,
Corporate Cultures

The literature on organizational change has its own vocabulary and is filled with references to "mission," "vision," and "values." The terms often seem to be used interchangeably, and confusion regarding them is common; however, understanding the relationships between mission, vision, and values is important in launching a school improvement initiative. Senge (1990) provides a useful analogy in his description of a healthy organization resting on a tripod. The first leg, mission, answers the question of "why" the organization exists. The second leg, vision, addresses the issue of "what" the organization is to become. The third leg, values, explains "how" the organization is to advance toward its ideal by promoting certain behavior and attitudes. A healthy organization requires a clear sense of all three of these important aspects of its life. The current emphasis on restructuring schools often gives a great deal of attention to developing a vision statement without addressing the important task of identifying the values that will drive the organization toward that vision. School improvement leaders must understand that an essential aspect of their leadership role is the identification, promotion, and protection of the values that will advance the school toward its vision.

The extent to which a vision statement affects a school depends in large part on the degree to which that vision is reflected in the core values chosen as the benchmark for decision making. These values represent the *specific behaviors and attitudes* that must be demonstrated within the organization on a day-to-day basis if it is to make progress toward its desired future state. The importance of values to an organization has been cited again and again. Peter Senge (1990, 224-5) observed:

> Values answer the question, "How do we want to act along the path toward achieving our vision?"....Core values are necessary to help people with day-to-day decision making.... But core values are only helpful if they can be translated into concrete behaviors.

Warren Bennis and Burt Nanus (1985) found that explicit, widely held organizational values provide a context of meaning to the members of an organization, helping them to know how they are expected to behave. An understanding of these values enables the members of the organization to make decisions without frequent appeals to higher levels because they know what results are required. Peters and Waterman (1982, 280) also placed great emphasis on the important role that values play in excellent organizations. They wrote, "Every excellent company we studied is clear on what it stands for, and takes the process of value shaping seriously. In fact, we wonder whether it is possible to be an excellent company without clarity on values and without having the right sort of values." Terry Deal and Allan Kennedy (1982, 11) observed:

> In our work and study we have found that successful companies place a great deal of emphasis on values. In general these companies share three characteristics:

- They stand for something, that is, they have a clear and explicit philosophy about how they aim to conduct their business.
- Management pays a great deal of attention to shaping and fine tuning these values to conform to the economic and business environment of the company and to communicating them to the organization.
- These values are known and shared by all the people who work for the company, from the lowliest production worker right through to the rank of senior management.

Paraphrasing Deal and Kennedy, the following can be ascribed to excellent schools:

- They stand for something, that is, they have a clear and explicit philosophy or vision, a shared sense of purpose, and a common view of what makes for excellent schooling.
- The leaders of the district and individual schools pay a great deal of attention both to shaping a shared set of values that reflect and promote

the vision of an excellent school and to communicating these values throughout the school district.

• These values are known and shared by all of those who work in the schools, from support personnel right through to the superintendent and board of education.

In her review of the current literature on organizational effectiveness, Cathy Enz (1986) identified the power of shared values as one of the most prevalent themes. The message from these studies to school practitioners is consistent and unequivocal. If a school is to become an excellent organization, those within it must be guided by core values that grow out of the shared vision. Whereas vision represents the long-term target, values direct the daily efforts toward that target.

What are some core values that best reflect a commitment to excellence? In examining the dominant beliefs of the companies they describe in *In Search of Excellence*, Peters and Waterman (1982, 285) found these few basic values were consistently present in excellent organizations:

1. belief in the best

2. belief in the importance of the details of execution, the nuts and bolts of doing the job well

3. belief in the importance of people as individuals

4. belief in superior quality and service

5. belief that most members of the organization should be innovators, and its corollary, the willingness to support failure

6. belief in the importance of informality to enhance communication

7. explicit belief in and recognition of the importance of economic growth and profits

The last of these values clearly is not pertinent to schools. However, if one substituted "explicit belief in and recognition of the importance of student academic achievement" for the last value, these values could easily be applied to a school.

One analysis (Schlechty, 1990) of the values essential to successful school improvement offered the following list:

1. a recognition of the importance of positive recognition and affirmation

2. a recognition of the importance of variety, both intellectual and professional

3. a recognition of the need to feel that what one does makes a difference and that doing things differently will make a difference as well

4. a recognition of the need for affiliation and collegial support and interaction

TRANSLATING VISION INTO VALUES

When a faculty describes the school it seeks to create, a dream is put in motion. There is a sense of optimism, hope, and focus. But this vision of the future generates a new question. What are the beliefs, attitudes, and behaviors that a faculty must exhibit if the vision of the school is to be advanced? In other words, what values must a faculty agree to promote, protect, and defend if the school is to move toward its vision? One school dealt with the task of identifying its core values by creating a task force. After the school community described the vision it was striving to achieve (as outlined in Chapter Two), the task force extracted from the vision statement a list of teacher behaviors and attitudes that were necessary to help that ideal become a reality. The task force then presented these values to the entire faculty for consideration. After considerable discussion, the faculty endorsed the following statement of principles:

1. We will teach to the course objectives and provide evidence of student achievement of those objectives.

2. We will make full use of the instructional time allotted to us.

3. We will demonstrate our belief and expectation that all students can achieve the objectives of the courses to which they are assigned.

4. We will help to ensure an orderly atmosphere that is conducive to learning throughout the building.

5. We will treat all members of the school community with respect.

Several characteristics of this list are particularly noteworthy. First, it is brief. The longer the litany of "thou shalts," the less likely it is to be remembered by teachers and thus the less likely it is to be effective in guiding them. Second, it is results-oriented in that it addresses the issue of student achievement and emphasizes that teachers must continually weigh their efforts in terms of impact on student achievement. Third, it gives direction to the daily decisions and activities of teachers. A pious platitude such as "we will recognize the spark of divinity that flows from the soul of every child" is of very little help to teachers. Each statement carries explicit expectations regarding the responsibilities of teachers. Finally, it provides for large measures of autonomy for the individual teacher. Although instruction must be directed to particular student outcomes, the teacher is left free to determine how he or she will see to it that students achieve those outcomes.

Another faculty agreed to the following value statements as the guideline for their behavior and decisions:

1. We will identify and teach to explicit outcomes by grade level.

2. We will frequently assess student mastery of outcomes in a variety of ways and will provide students with many opportunities to demonstrate mastery of those concepts.

3. We will seek not only to be understood, but also to understand through frequent communications with students, parents, and colleagues.

4. We will work collaboratively in developing instructional strategies, designing methods of assessment, and advancing the vision of the school.

5. We will involve parents and the community at-large in the learning process by creating shared learning experiences.

6. We will model the self-discipline, self-motivation, and commitment to high quality work that we hope to develop in our students.

7. We will help to insure an orderly atmosphere that is conducive to learning.

8. We will treat all members of the school community with dignity and respect.

The lists provided here are meant to serve as examples, not as models. Each school should establish its own unique statement of values and should involve the entire faculty in the process of identifying those values. Representative parents and students also should be included in a process to draft value statements for their respective groups. For example, the student leaders of one school wrote and adopted the core values for students that are listed below.

We believe that the likelihood of a student's success and satisfaction is increased significantly if he or she:

1) conducts himself/herself in a manner that contributes to an orderly atmosphere and ensures the rights of others

2) is considerate of others—teachers, staff, fellow students, visitors, etc.

3) becomes involved in the extracurricular programs of the school

4) gives his/her best effort to all academic and co-curricular pursuits

Value statements for parents might include the following:

- I will establish high expectations for my student. I will not accept minimum effort or indifference to quality work.
- I will know what is expected in each of my student's classes.
- I will insist on good attendance.
- I will provide a quiet place and time in our home for study.
- I will encourage my student to become actively involved in the co-curricular program of the school.
- I will be actively involved in the school and supportive of its work.
- I will express my appreciation to school staff members who go above and beyond the call of duty.
- I will model the importance of life-long learning.

Those who attempt to develop value statements for the different segments of the school community are almost always certain to observe an interesting phenomenon. Each group will have little difficulty in identifying the values that the other group should observe in order to improve the school. Administrators are adept at pointing out the behavior and attitudes that are desirable for teachers, teachers can readily identify what parents can do to improve schools, etc. The challenge, however, is to get each group to focus on itself and what it can do to improve the school.

Once again, the key to the effectiveness of explicit value statements in influencing the behaviors within an organization is the degree to which they are understood and endorsed. Value statements that are imposed simply will not work in the long run. In fact, value shaping can be dysfunctional when the values are imposed rather than emergent. Those who seek to bring about school improvement must take great care not to sacrifice shared commitment on the altar of expedience and efficiency.

PLANNING FOR SCHOOL IMPROVEMENT

Developing detailed improvement plans is an important aspect of translating values from word into action. If the talk about school improvement is not translated into behavior, then discouragement, pessimism, and cynicism will emerge. Developing specific plans for improvement should quickly follow the identification of vision and values. The creation of specific improvement plans is the organization's way of demonstrating a genuine commitment to vision and values.

There are many ways to develop school improvement plans. The following is one that is easily adaptable to virtually any school or school district.

Step One: Where Are We Now?

The first step in developing school improvement plans is to assess the current state of the school or school district in relation to the vision and values that have been developed. The assessment should focus on specific characteristics, with the school's vision and values serving as the benchmarks against which the school is measured. Depending on the time and resources available, data-gathering procedures may range from conducting fairly simple surveys of opinion to compiling a complex array of statistics. The following are some commonly used means of assessing school practices.

- *Faculty and Parent Perception Surveys.* There are many excellent instruments available for surveying the perceptions of faculty and parents. These survey instruments usually are developed around the findings of research on effective schools. However, one problem with these instruments is that the survey items may not adequately reflect all of the characteristics of excellent schooling that a particular school has identified. Therefore, the instruments need to be adapted to fit a particular school's set of values.

- *Interviews.* The data gathered from the faculty and parent surveys often reflect broad patterns of perception. Follow-up interviews should be conducted in order to get more specific, in-depth responses. The interview questions should be developed after the data from the survey instruments have been analyzed and should be designed to solicit elaboration about specific areas of the school program. One Midwestern school district coordinated the interview sessions with a parent/teacher association meeting. Letters sent to the parents beforehand explained the purpose of the interviews, told how long they would take, and gave a few sample questions. At the PTA meeting, interviewers were available in various rooms throughout the school. This procedure worked for the particular district because it was well planned and there was an excellent communication between the school district and those being interviewed.

- *Observations.* It is helpful to send observers into schools periodically to get information that did not emerge from the surveys and interviews. Data recorded by observers also can be used to validate the survey and interview responses. The observations should be informal and naturalistic. Training of observers need not be extensive, since the observations are not research-oriented in the strictest sense. Observers should be given some guidance as to what should be observed, such as traffic flow between classes, classroom teaching, cafeteria services, or attendance at club meetings. Observers should take detailed notes, recording only what they see and hear and not their feelings about what they observe.

Schools that are assessing themselves do not always utilize observational data. However, the information gained from observations of the school's day-to-day operation can complement the other data collected.

- *Examples of Student Work.* Another important source of information is student performance data. Information should certainly include data on student performance on criterion-referenced and standardized tests. It should not, however, be limited to test scores, because the quality of students' work often cannot be determined solely from standardized tests. Exhibitions of student work, analysis of student portfolios, and oral examinations are important if an accurate portrait of the state of the school is to be developed.

There are many other assessment methods available. The methods used are not crucial; what matters is that data are gathered about the school as it exists before school improvement plans are developed. Information on the state of the school will provide the baseline for developing plans and measuring programs. The quality of improvement plans will depend to a great degree on the quality of data collection and analysis during this step of the planning process.

Step Two: Where Are We Going?

Once those involved in the school improvement effort have reached agreement about the school's vision and values and assessed the current status of the school in relation to those benchmarks, it is time for the next step. Step two is to bridge the gap between "where we want to be" and "where we are" by setting improvement goals for each of the categories in the school's statement of values.

The development of widely understood and widely accepted goals is critical in the school improvement process. Healthy organizations are goal driven, and their goals reflect the central values of the organization. In fact, goal development is one of the most visible ways to institutionalize the values of an organization. Effective goals give clear directions, maintain a unity of purpose, and advance organizational and personal visions. As Garfield (1986, 271) concluded, "Goals are dreams with deadlines."

A statement of goals for improvement should include: 1) an outline of specific plans for closing the gap between the current condition of the school and its ideal future state, 2) specific identification of responsibilities for carrying out the plan 3) a timetable for implementation, 4) the strategies and criteria to be used in evaluating the degree to which the goal has been achieved, and 5) priorities.

It is important to recognize that not all of the gaps can be closed at once. Some gaps are wider and more complex than others and thus may cost more and take more time to bridge. Improvement plans should be multi-year plans that set priorities as to what is to be accomplished in year one, two, three, and so on. There seems to be widespread agreement that significant school improvement requires more than one or two years. The quick fix just does not work. Setting priorities and *persistently* pursuing long-range goals are crucial aspects of a school improvement effort.

It is important that school improvement plans be reasonable. One of the reasons people fail to maintain their own personal renewal efforts is the same reason many school improvement efforts fail — the plans are unrealistic from the start. Most effective change takes place in small increments over a long period of time. It is much better to have a long string of small successes that begin to build a culture of excellence than to have gigantic flops from which it is virtually impossible to recover. Developing plans that are reasonable requires 1) an accurate assessment of both the problems and the resources that are required to resolve them, and 2) a clear understanding of both the characteristics of personnel and the resources likely to be available.

Improvement plans should help people to identify not only where the school is going, but also exactly how it will get there. To communicate this message effectively, plans need to be clear, concise, specific, and as simple as possible. Plans must be understood by those who make things happen. Some people have the tendency to equate the quality of improvement plans with their complexity, but this tendency must be avoided at all cost!

Finally, plans should be made public and should be presented with a sense of optimism and enthusiasm. A public announcement of goals communicates commitment to school improvement efforts.

An effective structure for the development of effective improvement plans is the task force or "adhocracy" (Waterman, 1990). Unlike standing committees, which often meet for the sake of meeting and postpone decisions because another meeting is always scheduled, the task force functions as a short-term, problem-solving work group. Typically composed of three to seven members who are given the clear and visible support of the organization's leadership, they are large enough to represent the affected constituencies yet small enough to get work done efficiently. The groups work best when they avoid pouncing on a solution and instead proceed in a structured way to state the problem, formulate one or more hypotheses, gather and analyze facts, pose alternatives until a solution begins to emerge, and then serve as champions for their recommendations. The goal of a task force is not the presentation of a report, but the identification of recommendations that will bring about change. One of the benefits of the adhocracy approach to planning is that it allows for widespread participation in the school improvement effort and broadly dispersed leadership opportunities. Furthermore, the structure is designed to stimulate innovation.

Cautions Regarding the Use of Adhocracy

The adhocracy strategy can be overused or used badly. In some instances, over-eager administrators have attempted to demonstrate their endorsement of this small-group, participatory process by convening task forces to consider the most trivial of issues. Surveys of teachers have consistently revealed that although teachers want to be included in discussions of substantive issues, they have no desire to be included in every decision. In other cases administrators have failed to provide members with a clear purpose and well-defined parameters. Yet another error is the practice of assigning responsibilities to a group but failing to provide its members with the support and authority to fulfill them.

How can these problems be avoided? "Participation," wrote Kanter (1983, 243)..."needs to be managed just as carefully as any other organization system." She suggested that group involvement in solving problems and making decisions is inappropriate in the following situations:

- when one person clearly has greater expertise on the subject than all others
- when those affected by the decision acknowledge and accept the expertise
- when there is an obviously correct answer
- when someone has the topic as part of his or her regular job and it was not his or her idea to form the group
- when no one really cares all that much about the issue
- when no development or learning important to others would be served by their involvement
- when there is a need to act quickly
- when people work more happily and productively alone.

In short, the adhocracy strategy represents a useful tool in a systematic school improvement effort and is congruent with the proposals for restructuring that are currently in fashion. However, the strategy can be used inappropriately. Like most of the ideas that hold promise for school improvement, it must be considered within a particular context rather than applied uniformly.

STRATEGIES FOR ESTABLISHING AND MAINTAINING VALUES

Leaders of outstanding schools and school districts take the necessary steps to make sure that the vision and values of the school are reflected in its day-to-day operation. They develop specific, simple school improvement plans with goals that are specifically intended to advance vision and values. The following strategies are recommended to assist school improvement efforts through the identification and utilization of core values.

1. Create a task force to lead faculty-wide discussions aimed at identifying the behaviors and attitudes the faculty must demonstrate in order to advance the vision of the school. Continue these discussions until there is consensus.

2. Create task forces for students and parents to develop a process for arriving at the values for their respective groups that are essential for improving the school. Once again the process should result in consensus and widespread support for the values.

3. Highlight the values in faculty manuals, student handbooks, parent handbooks, and any other available school publication. Remember that values cannot influence behavior if people are unaware of them.

4. Insist that all staff remain within the parameters of the agreed-on values, but otherwise provide them with large measures of autonomy in their day-to-day tasks.

5. Develop goals and plans for school improvement that are directed toward promoting the agreed-on values.

6. Develop systematic procedures for monitoring the presence of the values in the school.

7. Demonstrate genuine support for the values by confronting behavior and attitudes that are contrary to them.

8. Promote the values by recognizing administrators, teachers, parents, and students whose behavior and attitudes serve as examples of the values. (See Chapter Nine.)

4

The Principal as a Leader

*If a school is a vibrant, innovative,
child-centered place; if it has a
reputation for excellence in teaching; if
students are performing to the best of
their ability; one can almost always
point to the principal's leadership as
the key to success.*

—U.S. Senate Resolution 359, (1970)

*Managers do things right. Leaders do
the right things.*

—Warren Bennis and Burt Nanus,
Leaders

O ne of the most consistent findings of the research on both excellent
businesses and effective schools is the importance of strong leadership. Warren Bennis and Burt Nanus argued that organizations cannot be
successful without effective leadership, which they describe as "the key
factor in the ability of business to translate its vision into reality" (1985,
20). Even Tom Peters and Robert Waterman, who insisted that excellent
companies achieve their excellence through the extraordinary efforts of
ordinary people, acknowledged that these companies "have been truly
blessed with unusual leadership" (1982, 81–82).

The research on effective schools focuses particularly on the leadership
of the principal. After visiting schools across the country, Jane Eisner
reported, "The key to a school's success is the 'principal principle': the
notion that a strong administrator with vision and with ability to carry out
his or her goals can make an enormous difference in a school" (1979, 59).
Another study (Goldhammer and Becker, 1972) concluded that excellent
schools inevitably are led by aggressive, professionally alert, dynamic
principals determined to provide the kind of educational program they
deem necessary. Ron Edmonds (1979, 22) argued that one of the most
tangible and indispensable characteristics of effective schools is "strong

administrative leadership without which the disparate elements of good schooling can neither be brought together nor kept together." Even Stewart Purkey and Marshall Smith, (1983, 443) who described their orientation to the effective schools research as skeptical and admitted that they were "suspicious of the 'Great Principal' theory," acknowledged that "it seems clear that leadership is necessary to initiate and maintain the improvement process . . . [and] the principal is uniquely positioned to fill this role."

What is the role of the principal? Some descriptions of that role characterize the principal as a frontline supervisor, whereas others portray the principal as a middle manager. Some authors describe the principalship in terms of its functions — school-community relations, staff evaluation, educational program development, and business and building management. Others describe the principalship in terms of the various publics with whom the principal must work: staff, students, parents, other administrators, and the general public. However, recent research on effective organizations, effective leaders, and effective schools calls for a new definition of the principalship, one that recognizes the four major roles of the principal:

1. empowerer of teachers

2. promoter and protector of values

3. instructional leader

4. manager of climate

In short, the effective principal must be both a leader and a manager. As a leader, the principal must empower teachers, promote and protect the values of the school, and monitor and evaluate instructional effectiveness. As a manager, the principal must work to maintain a climate that is both productive and satisfying. This chapter will consider the principal as leader. Chapter Five will focus upon managing organizational climate

THE BASIC DILEMMA: STRONG PRINCIPAL OR AUTONOMOUS TEACHERS?

The research on both effective principals and effective schools cites the importance of principals who serve as strong instructional leaders and who closely monitor student achievement. Various studies have described effective principals as forceful, dynamic, assertive, energetic, and quick to assume the initiative. Good principals take charge and strive to make the school over in their own image. They help give a school an image of what it can be and then provide the drive, support, and skills to make that image a reality. It is almost impossible to read this research without visualizing aggressive principals who roam their schools with a clear vision and the determination to achieve it regardless of the obstacles.

The research on motivation seems to offer a distinctly different message to school administrators. Frederick Herzberg (1966) conducted 17 different empirical studies of diverse work groups to determine which factors were effective in inspiring unusual commitment and effort on the part of employees. Herzberg found that although factors such as salary, security, working conditions, and interpersonal relations could lead to worker dissatisfaction, they were ineffective in motivating individuals above and beyond the call of duty. Employees were inspired to exceptional dedication only when they believed in the significance of their work and felt a sense of recognition, responsibility, achievement, and advancement as a result of their efforts. Herzberg concluded that these motivational factors were best promoted by job enrichment, a management strategy that requires supervisors to yield or at least share some of their decision-making authority and give greater autonomy and responsibility to employees.

Thomas Sergiovanni (1967) applied Herzberg's research model to teachers with strikingly similar results. In his survey of more than 3,000 teachers, Sergiovani found that although the notion of advancement is not a factor in teacher job satisfaction, the feelings of achievement, recognition, and responsibility that go with increased autonomy in the classroom are the most significant factors in teacher satisfaction.

More recent studies of high-performing and innovative companies have yielded similar findings and led to the conclusion that organizations should "empower" their employees by giving them the opportunity to act on their ideas. Peters and Waterman (1982) found that the best-run companies are able to inspire extraordinary commitment by extending a large measure of autonomy to their individual employees. Workers in these companies, given the freedom to determine some of their goals and the autonomy to develop strategies to achieve them, consistently outperformed their more rigidly supervised counterparts again and again. Almost without exception, the best-run companies have shifted the concept of the employee from one who carries out orders to one who takes responsibility and initiative, monitors his or her own work, and uses supervisors as facilitators and consultants. They have realized that the people who know the most about any job are those doing it.

The message this body of research sends to educators is clear: Give teachers more freedom in what they teach and how they teach it, and both their morale and their performance will improve. This is, in fact, the basis of the recommendations for educational reform offered by the advocates of school restructuring. For example, the Carnegie Foundation's Forum on Education and the Economy (1986) called for reforms that would empower teachers and transform schools from bureaucratic, hierarchical societies into collegial communities in which teachers are treated as professionals and assumed to have the expertise needed to decide how best to do their jobs. In fact, the Carnegie report suggests that perhaps the position of principal is no longer essential. A publication of the United States Department of Education designed to promote school restructuring (National LEADership Network, 1991) advocated giving teachers increased authority and responsibility for the teaching and learning environment and suggested that school-based teams of teachers should use shared decision-making processes to resolve significant issues.

The seemingly contradictory messages of the research on effective schools and the research on motivation and organizational effectiveness have presented a dilemma for conscientious principals. The message from the effective schools research seems to be "Take charge! Be a leader not a manager! Push and pull and prod until your personal vision of the school becomes a reality." The research on motivation offers very different advice: "Empower your teachers! Give them the freedom and autonomy that will enable them to fulfill their personal and professional needs." What's a principal to do? What style of leadership is best suited for a school interested in advancing toward its ideal?

CHOOSING ONE AT THE EXPENSE OF THE OTHER

Many school administrators attempt to resolve the dilemma by subscribing to one school of research and ignoring the other. The administration of a nationally recognized high school has made a serious effort to apply the research on effective schools and its emphasis on monitoring student achievement. Administrators have established elaborate curriculum guides for each course, complete with specific objectives and unit examinations that assess student mastery of each objective. All instructors teaching the same course are required to follow the same day-by-day course outline. These teachers also administer identical unit tests on the same day, according to a testing calendar established by the administration. The tests are scored and results recorded in the testing center of the school, and thus administrators are able to monitor student achievement course by course and teacher by teacher. It is difficult to conceive of a more thorough monitoring of student achievement.

But what impact does this system have on classroom teachers? They are robbed of their professionalism by the assembly-line mentality that characterizes this approach to instruction. They have little say about what is taught and virtually no opportunity to make decisions in such critical areas as pacing, reteaching, or assessment. Decisions regarding the complex task of teaching are made by individuals far removed from the classroom.

Meanwhile, other administrators have responded to the findings of the research on motivation by opting for a hands-off policy toward their staffs as the best means of ensuring autonomy and, therefore, high teacher morale. One prominent midwestern school district provides an excellent example of this *laissez-faire* approach to administration. There is no district-level curriculum in the school system, and thus each teacher is allowed to determine the content of his or her courses. Members of the same department who are teaching the same course are under no obligation to coordinate their efforts; they can decide independently what they will include and emphasize in that course. Once a teacher is awarded tenure in the district, he or she is free from the demands of formal observation and evaluation. Teachers know that after they achieve tenure they will never again have their classrooms visited by an administrator for the purpose of assessing instruction. The only school-wide monitoring of student achievement that takes place is analysis of the performance of each graduating class on the ACT exam.

The administrators in this district take pride in the fact that they have enacted policies that provide academic freedom for each teacher. Indeed, it is difficult to imagine a school in which teachers have more autonomy in the area of instruction. Although one might anticipate that job satisfaction and teacher morale would flourish in such an atmosphere, a conversation with a veteran member of the faculty revealed otherwise. "We are told that the administration is determined to safeguard academic freedom, but to many of us it just comes across as administrative indifference," he admitted. "It seems as if no one but me cares how much or how well the kids learn in my class. It has been years since I have had any feedback on my teaching. I think many of us feel neglected, ignored. I know I'd like some recognition for my efforts in the classroom, and no one in this school except my students is in a position to give me that recognition."

The Solution: Directed Autonomy

The solution to the dilemma of strong principal versus autonomous teachers is for the principal to be both an inflexible, autocratic protector of values and an enthusiastic empowerer of teachers. This solution is described by Waterman (1987, 82) as "directed autonomy." When this concept is applied, an organization identifies a few central values that will give direction to the activities and decisions of all its members and then demands rigid adherence to these few non-negotiable values on the part of its members. At the same time, however, it promotes and encourages individual innovation and autonomy in day-to-day operations. This approach allows leaders of an organization to emphasize the importance of control and freedom at the same time. Those who adhere to the principles of directed autonomy regard every staff member as a source of creative input.

Schools that follow the dictates of directed autonomy have been characterized as both tightly and loosely coupled. On the one hand, there exists a strong sense of core values that define the parameters of behavior and are vigilantly promoted and protected. On the other hand, teachers are given a great deal of freedom as to how these values are to be realized (Sergiovanni, 1984).

For the most part school administrators have not responded warmly to the calls for increased teacher empowerment. Even though the National Association of Secondary School Principals endorsed "substantial decentralization of decision-making authority" and supported the contention that "enlightened organizations include staff members in the decision-making processes" (Ventures, p.6), principals have often demonstrated a reluctance to move empowerment from rhetoric to practice. A survey ("Teachers", 1986) of more than 8,500 teachers revealed that only 28% of them could be classified as empowered. More that 85% of the respondents believed that quality of instruction would improve if they were allowed to increase their involvement in curriculum decisions. Only 30% of teachers reported being involved in textbook decisions, and 80% said they were never consulted about who gets hired in the school.

For many school administrators, the concept of empowerment is difficult to reconcile with their image of an instructional leader. They genuinely fear a loss of control. However, this difficulty is based on a muddled view of both empowerment and leadership. These individuals confuse leadership with being "the boss." The real issue that should preoccupy principals is not, "Who is in control?" but rather, "How can we best get results?" Giving teachers an opportunity to exercise their judgment serves two practical and powerful purposes toward this end. First, it promotes greater density of leadership. Vitality in a school depends upon the willingness of a great many people within it to take the initiative in identifying and solving problems. As the former director of the Harvard University Principal's Center (Barth, 1990, 123) wrote:

> If the principal tries to do it all, much of it will be left undone by anyone...the principal gains influence and demonstrates leadership by entrusting some of it to others. It has become increasingly important to share leadership and to no longer even aspire to fully understand and control every aspect of the school.

The willingness to assume responsibility is the very essence of leadership. As principals are able to persuade others to assume responsibility, they expand the base of leadership within their schools.

Second, empowerment eliminates excuses for failure to perform. People cannot blame failure on the decisions of others when they are free to determine how to complete a task. When a group of teachers works together to determine the curriculum of a course and its intended outcomes, the textbooks and materials to be used, the appropriate instructional strategies and pacing, and the best methods of assessing student achievement, it is difficult for those teachers to blame poor results on others. Although principals who empower their teaching staffs may indeed give up a degree of control in some areas, they do so in order to gain control over what really matters — results.

Administrators must recognize that power given is power gained. They must recognize that their own power is amplified by the presence of powerful, capable colleagues. They must recognize that by developing, rewarding, and recognizing those around them, they are "simply allowing the human assets with which they work to appreciate in value" (Garfield, 182). They must recognize that the more they empower, the more they can achieve and the more successful the whole enterprise can become. They must be willing to break from the bureaucratic, hierarchical structure that has characterized public schooling and develop the skills that are essential to successful empowerment — delegating, stretching the abilities of others, and encouraging educated risk taking.

Following are some specific ideas for increasing teacher involvement in various areas.

1. *Developing the curriculum.* Chapter Six discusses a process for establishing a focused, school-wide curriculum. It is based upon the premise that the teachers who will be responsible for delivering a curriculum should play a major role in its development. All teachers of a given grade or subject should be called on to arrive at a consensus as to what student outcomes should be achieved in that grade or subject and then should be held accountable for achieving those outcomes.

2. *Selecting instructional materials.* It seems obvious that the teachers who will use particular textbooks, equipment, and materials should have the major voice in their selection. But, the idea that decisions should be turned over to the people who must do the work is both disarmingly simple and seldom put into practice.

3. *Determining instructional styles and strategies.* Although a principal can and should establish parameters for classroom instruction (for example, teachers will teach to the specified student outcomes, will make full use of the instructional period, and will ensure that all students are actively engaged in the lesson), those parameters should stop short of mandating particular teaching styles. Some teachers thrive on individualized instruction, others are proponents of cooperative learning in small groups, and still others are both more comfortable and more successful

with large-group instruction. Forcing a particular mode of instruction on teachers robs them of both their professionalism and the autonomy they need to be effective. Certainly teachers should be encouraged to expand their repertoire and attempt to develop new skills. Certainly principals should discourage teaching behaviors that are inconsistent with the findings of the research on effective teaching. However, it is the results of teaching that should concern principals, not the style. Day-to-day instructional decisions should remain with the teacher.

4. *Scheduling.* Scheduling is a bone of contention at virtually all levels of public schooling. Elementary teachers grouse about who gets which students and about having students pulled out of their classrooms for special programs in art, music, reading, and so on. High school teachers compare class sizes and number of preparations and scrutinize who gets assigned to teach which course. Why shouldn't teachers be invited to make these decisions collectively? Not only would they better understand the difficulties inherent in scheduling, but their collective deliberations might result in workable ways of resolving some of those difficulties. They are certainly likely to feel better about a teaching schedule that they had a hand in fashioning than about one imposed on them.

5. *Assessing student achievement.* Teachers should play a key role in developing the strategies for monitoring school-wide achievement. If locally developed tests are to be used, teachers should work collectively to develop them. If standardized achievement tests are to be used, teachers should help select the tests that best fit the school curriculum. If alternative assessment strategies are to be used (for example, writing folders, portfolios, or rating scales), teachers should be primarily responsible for developing the specifics of those strategies.

6. *Planning and presenting staff-development programs.* In most schools, if teachers are involved in the planning of the staff-development program at all, their involvement is limited to a survey of their interest in potential topics. Too often administrators select both the staff development topic and those who will present the topic to a passive teaching staff. However, one innovative school system demonstrated the role teachers can play in staff development. The principal established certain parameters for the staff development program:

a. Several options or themes had to be offered.

b. Options had to be based on teacher interests.

c. Each option had to provide for ongoing training.

d. The training had to include an opportunity to learn, practice, and receive feedback on a new skill.

    e. Faculty members who were not interested in any of the themes
could propose their own individual or small group staff-development plan.

A faculty steering committee was then invited to assume responsibility
for the planning and delivery of the program. The committee polled the
faculty several times to identify five themes that were of interest to a
significant number of teachers. Faculty members who were recognized as
having particular interest or expertise in these five areas were then invited
to work in teams of two or three to develop the program in that area. These
teams assumed full responsibility for all of the decisions regarding their
programs. Each team had to decide how it would make colleagues aware
of the objectives and activities of its program, what funding would be
required and how it would be allocated, whether to use local or outside
speakers and resources, what materials would be required, and how the
effectiveness of the program would be evaluated. The principal provided
each team with support, time for planning, an adequate budget, and
encouragement.

There are several benefits to this approach to staff development. First,
it gives individual teachers an opportunity to pursue particular topics or
develop their own improvement programs. Second, since teachers have a
better understanding of the interest and needs of their colleagues than do
the administrators who typically plan staff development, the programs
they develop are more likely to be relevant. Finally, by giving recognition
and responsibility to individual teachers, the program provides a means
of developing leadership potential among the faculty.

7. *Hiring new staff.* Teachers should play a role in interviewing and
selecting colleagues, particularly if they will be called on to work closely
with the new staff members. If teachers at a particular grade level or in a
particular subject are expected to coordinate their efforts, they deserve an
opportunity to participate in the process of selecting new team members.

8. *Mentoring.* One of the most important factors in the success of any
organization is its effectiveness in helping new members understand its
culture, or more simply, how things are done. Teachers new to a school
have always believed, and rightly so, that the best source of this type of
information is other teachers. Nevertheless, the formal programs that
administrators have developed to orient and acculturize new faculty have
consistently failed to utilize veteran teachers.

Mentoring programs offer a solution. Each new teacher is assigned a
mentor, who is then responsible for teaching the new-comer "how we do
things around here." The mentors provide instruction and advice in
virtually all areas of the school's operation, from such mundane matters
as how chalk is ordered to such substantive issues as how student achieve-

ment is assessed. Mentors introduce their new charges to the school's teacher evaluation program by observing them in the classroom and giving them feedback on their teaching performance. This peer coaching takes place before formal evaluation procedures by the administration.

9. *Serving on school improvement task forces.* Teachers should be encouraged to view the school in a context that goes beyond their individual classrooms. Senge (1990) describes the tendency to focus on one's own position within an organization as one of the "learning disabilities" that lead to the decline of the organization. This myopic point of view leads individuals to forget the larger purpose of the enterprise and lose a personal sense of responsibility for seeing to it that the larger purpose is achieved. Having teachers serve on task forces that make decisions about school improvement not only will result in better decisions but also will serve to remind teachers of the greater mission of the school.

What Empowerment Is Not

It is important to remember that empowerment is not simply turning people loose and hoping for the best. Being an advocate of empowering the work force is not synonymous with laissez-faire leadership. As Kanter (1983, 248) said, "Freedom is not the absence of structure, letting employees go off and do whatever they want, but rather a clear structure which enables people to work within established boundaries in a creative and autonomous way." Thus the principal who sets out to empower his or her teachers must, at the same time, demand that the values of the school be observed and continuously monitor the progress the school is making in realizing its vision.

The image of principal as both a relentless, autocratic protector of values and a transformational leader seeking new ways to empower teachers is somewhat paradoxical. However, the ability to conceptualize and manage this paradox is a key to successful leadership. Schools must be both loose and tight; principals must both encourage innovation and insist on compliance.

The concept of directed autonomy has much to offer school leaders. A school that has identified a few core values that are effective in giving direction to the daily activities of the staff is able to resolve the dilemma of strong administrative leadership versus teacher autonomy.

THE PRINCIPAL AS PROMOTER AND PROTECTOR OF VALUES

In the first several chapters it was argued that schools seeking excellence should base their efforts on explicit, widely understood statements of vision and values. The articulation of vision and values, however, will not have a significant impact on schools unless their principals accept the promotion and protection of those values as one of their essential responsibilities. In order to fulfill that responsibility, principals must both know what they want and communicate what they want to others in the school.

Effective Leaders Know What They Want

In his Pulitzer Prize-winning study of leadership, James McGregor Burns (1978) advised that the first step a leader must take in order to influence others is to clarify his or her own goals. It is impossible for an organization to remain focused on its vision and values unless its leaders are certain of what the vision and values entail. In short, leaders must know what they want to accomplish. Such clarity of purpose is particularly important in public schools, which have been called on to cure every ill and solve every social problem. Too often state legislatures or boards of education send the message that everything is important. As a result, nothing is done well.

Effective Leaders Communicate What They Want

Vision and values can influence an organization and those within it only if the vision and values are communicated. Mastery of communication is essential to effective leadership.

What are the keys to communication that attract and inspire? Peters and Waterman (1982, 83) discovered that one key is redundancy, a "boorish consistency over long periods of time in support of . . . one or two transcending values." Unlike most school administrators, who begin each school year with an explanation of what is new in the way of procedures and policies, effective principals will emphasize what remains the same, the vision and values that direct the efforts of those within their schools. Furthermore, effective principals will repeat that message at every opportunity, recognizing that, in the words of Peters and Waterman (1982, 83), "no opportunity is too small, no forum too insignificant, no audience too junior."

Bennis and Nanus (1985) cited the effective use of metaphors and slogans as another element in effective communication. Their advice to anyone trying to institute change is to ask, "How clear is the metaphor?" The principal of one high school that has made academic achievement its primary emphasis has a knack for including the school's slogan, "Where Minds Matter Most," in both written and oral communication. The principal of an elementary school committed to Sizer's notion that autonomy is the key to effective teaching coined the slogan "Student Achievement Through Teacher Empowerment" to help teachers and parents understand that commitment. A leader of a school that calls on teachers and students to give their best effort to enable the school to achieve excellence might adopt the slogan "Doing Our Best to Be the Best."

It is, however, the actions of leaders, not their exhortations or slogans, that communicate most clearly to others in the organization. In their study of effective business leadership, Tom Peters and Nancy Austin (1985) argued that simply paying attention to what is important is the most powerful means by which a leader can communicate to and influence others. Throughout their chapter on leadership, they repeated the message, "Attention is all there is." Leaders communicate both their expectations and their priorities through their observable behaviors.

Any assessment of a principal's effectiveness in communicating values should include the following questions:

1. *What does the principal plan for?* Does the principal develop long-term plans that are consistent with the vision of the school and are designed to instill its values? Does he or she share those plans with the staff and help them see the relationship between the plans and the mission? Does his or her daily planning provide an opportunity to concentrate on the factors that are most critical in advancing the school toward its vision?

2. *What does the principal monitor?* In most organizations, what gets monitored gets done. A principal who devotes considerable time and effort to the continual assessment of a particular condition within a school sends the message that the condition is important. Conversely, inattention to monitoring a particular factor indicates that the factor is less than essential, regardless of how often its importance is verbalized.

Often the values a principal communicates through monitoring contradict his or her professed values. The principal in one elementary school began the year with a speech urging teachers to embrace the district goal of improving student achievement. As an aside he admonished teachers for their overuse of the school copier during the previous year and insisted that they reduce the number of copies made for classroom use. An elaborate system was established to monitor the extent to which individual teachers were using the copy machine. Each time they used the machine, teachers were required to record their name, the date, what was being copied, how many copies were being made, and a brief explanation of why the copies were necessary. Every week a secretary would type a report based on the information from the log and present it to the principal. He, in turn, would record the results by teacher, keeping a running tally of the copies made by each. When a teacher was deemed to have been extravagant with the copier, that teacher was called before the principal and asked to mend his or her ways. Meanwhile, assessment of student achievement remained what it had always been, administration of a single standardized test, the results of which were presented to teachers without comment. The teachers in this school felt that the principal was communicating quite clearly what was really important to him.

3. *What does the principal model?* Several authorities define leadership in terms of how the leader behaves (Bellon, 1988). Principals who truly believe that the presence of certain values is critical to the success of their schools will attempt to model those values. A school that calls on teachers to be analytical regarding their own teaching efforts should have a principal who is both a thoughtful student of teaching and an analyst of his or her own leadership style. A school that asks teachers and students to be considerate of one another should have a principal who models consideration in his or her dealings with all members of the school community. A school that claims to value its teachers should have a principal who treats them as professionals. The research findings are compelling: effective principals use their own behavior to exemplify core values and reinforce those values through their daily routines (Deal and Peterson, 1990).

4. *What does the principal reinforce through recognition and celebration?* One of the most critical and powerful means of communicating and reinforcing values is constant attention to celebrating their presence within the organization. The importance of recognition and celebration has been cited repeatedly in the literature on effective business practices. Deal and Kennedy (1982) concluded that the values of an organization must be celebrated if they are to survive.

Recognition is a key to building the culture of pride that is found in excellent schools. A principal communicates values by recognizing and reinforcing those who act in accordance with those values. This public attention is important not only for the individual who receives it, but also for others in the organization who see that the things they might contribute will be noticed, applauded, and remembered.

Recognition must not be used indiscriminately, however. Brookover and his colleagues (1982, 84) observed that principals often recognize and praise teachers for factors unrelated to effective instruction, "for not bothering the principal or for doing other pleasant and desirable things, such as having an attractive room, being well dressed, or being the life of the Friday afternoon get together." Recognition simply for the sake of recognition serves no purpose in the effort to improve a school. Celebration of behaviors and attitudes that are disassociated with the values of the school will send messages that are at best confusing and at worst counterproductive. Celebration can be a powerful factor in promoting particular values within a school, but the principal must ensure that association between the celebration and the values is clear. (Chapter Nine is devoted to specific suggestions for celebrating the successes of a school.)

5. *What behavior is the principal willing to confront?* Although leaders in excellent companies encourage and reward individual autonomy, they insist that core values be observed and are willing to confront those who disregard such values. Their advocacy of these values may be described as rigid, non-negotiable, inflexible, and fanatical. Firings are generally the result not of poor performance but of the violation of values.

If principals wish to communicate the importance of particular values, they must be willing to confront those who disregard those values. If a school claims to value an orderly atmosphere throughout the building, the principal must be willing to confront the unruly student, the teacher who ignores misbehavior, or the parent who seeks to justify it. If a school claims to value teaching directed to particular student outcomes, the principal must be willing to confront the teacher whose instruction does not address those outcomes. If a school claims to value the best effort of teachers and students, the principal must be willing to confront those who give less.

Confrontation is not synonymous with personal attack, hostile discussion, or threats. Peters and Austin (1985, 373) described it as follows:

> ...a form of counseling in which the alternatives and consequences are clear and close at hand...a face-to-face meeting where you bring an individual's attention to the consequences of unacceptable performance....Confronting recognizes that a change is imperative.

Nevertheless, the word "confront" may seem jarring to principals who have traditionally been urged to promote a collegial, cooperative working relationship with their teachers. Furthermore, principals are people too and feel the basic human desire to have the approval and esteem of those with whom they work. Confrontation seems both anti-collegial and unlikely to result in the approval of the person who is challenged. But the principal who seeks to lead will place the values of the school above the desire for popularity. The ability to do without the constant approval and recognition of others is one of the keys to leadership. Burns (1978, 34) put it this way: "No matter how strong this yearning for unanimity... [leaders] must settle for far less than universal affection... They must accept conflict. They must be willing and able to be unloved."

Of course principals should not assume an adversarial relationship with their staffs. However, if the values of the school are to be communicated in a clear and unequivocal manner, principals must be willing to confront students, parents, or staff members when their conduct violates those values. Nothing will reduce the principal's credibility faster than the unwillingness to address an obvious problem.

Effective communication has little to do with eloquence. Principals can develop mastery of communication if they know what they want, deliver a consistent message with "boorish redundancy," and, above all else, ensure that their actions are congruent with the values they hope to communicate. They must remember the paraphrase of Emerson's observation: "What you do thunders above you so loudly that I can't hear what you say."

THE PRINCIPAL AS INSTRUCTIONAL LEADER

Studies of effective schools consistently cite the fact that such schools have principals who act as "strong instructional leaders." In one of the earliest and most widely cited studies, George Weber (1971) listed strong instructional leadership from the principal as one of eight school-wide characteristics that influenced student achievement. Studies by the New York Department of Education (1974), the Maryland State Department of Education (1978), Brookover and Lezotte (1979), and the California State Department of Education (1977) are among the many that have emphasized the critical importance of having a principal who acts as an instructional leader. Ron Edmonds (1979) found that one clear difference between improving and declining schools was that in the former principals acted as instructional leaders. James Lipham (1982, 15) went so far as to assert that "no change of substantial magnitude can occur in any school without their [principals'] understanding and support." It seems clear that much of the success of any school's effort to move toward its vision will depend on the instructional leadership of the principal.

But what does "instructional leadership" mean? What do principals do to demonstrate that they are instructional leaders? In its summary of the research on effective schools, the Northwest Regional Educational Laboratory (1990, 7-8) identified several behaviors that characterize instructional leadership:

- understanding the school's mission and stating it in direct, concrete terms in order to establish a focus and unify the staff
- portraying learning as the most important reason for being in school
- demonstrating the belief that all students can learn and that the school makes the difference between success and failure
- establishing standards and guidelines that can be used to monitor the effect of the curriculum
- protecting learning time from disruption and emphasizing the priority of efficient use of classroom time
- maintaining a safe, orderly school environment

- monitoring student progress by means of explicit performance data and sharing those data with the staff
- establishing incentives and rewards to encourage excellence in student and teacher performance
- allocating resources according to instructional priorities
- establishing procedures to guide parental involvement
- maintaining two-way communication with parents
- expressing the expectation that instructional programs improve over time
- involving staff and others in planning implementation strategies
- monitoring the implementation of new practices and programs
- celebrating the accomplishments of students, staff, and the school
- knowing, legitimizing, and applying research on effective instruction
- making frequent classroom visits to observe instruction
- focusing teacher supervision on instructional improvement

Providing Instructional Leadership Through Teacher Supervision

It is impossible for principals to function as instructional leaders unless they are willing to monitor teaching by venturing into the arena where instruction takes place: the classroom. Principals who do not choose to be instructional leaders often balk at the time commitment that is necessary to provide the kind of supervision that improves instruction, arguing that their managerial duties do not allow them to devote time to instructional improvement. Effective principals find the time. In his review of research on effective principals, Lipham (1982, 14) wrote, "Effective principals are skilled in time management and find opportunities to plan cooperatively with teachers, visit and observe classrooms, provide teachers with helpful feedback, and evaluate the progress of both staff and students."

In order to make time to provide meaningful supervision, a principal may have to persuade the local board of education that teachers should be formally evaluated every two or three years rather than annually. Research on adult learners indicates that they need an opportunity to practice and to receive timely feedback when they are attempting to acquire a new skill; thus an evaluation program in which teachers receive feedback three or four times in one year and then are not formally evaluated the next is superior to one in which they are visited only once each year.

In addition to spending considerable time in the classroom, instructional leaders develop the expertise necessary to assess the effectiveness of instruction. Principals must be sufficiently knowledgeable about effective teaching practices to provide teachers with meaningful feedback on their instructional strategies and methods. As Gordon Cawelti (1984, 3) concluded, "The difference between effective principals and others seems to lie in their knowledge of quality instruction." Currently, many principals have neither sufficient knowledge of the research on effective teaching nor adequate observation and conferencing skills to help teachers improve their instruction; but if schools are to move toward excellence, principals must take responsibility for developing such knowledge and skills.

Charles Garfield (1986) found that the peak performers of the business world have a sustained commitment to personal and professional growth and development. They identify what skills they need to be successful and assume responsibility for developing these capabilities. Principals who hope to lead a school in the pursuit of a vision must emulate these peak performers. They must recognize that if they are to be the instructional leaders that effective schools require, they must become students of good teaching, improve their classroom observation skills, and develop effective conferencing techniques. Subsequent chapters will offer suggestions in each of these areas and will outline an instructional supervision process designed to enable a principal to serve as both an empowerer of teachers and a strong instructional leader.

ENHANCING THE LEADERSHIP OF THE PRINCIPAL AND THE EMPOWERMENT OF TEACHERS

Following are some strategies recommended to principals interested in enhancing both their own leadership and the empowerment of teachers:

1. Play a key role in identifying and stating in writing the key values of the school.

2. Replace the rules and regulations in the faculty manual with the school's statement of values.

3. Initiate discussions of the school's statement of values with individual teachers. Can they articulate these values? If not, you have work to do.

4. Review your long-term and short-term goals. Does your planning reflect the values of the school?

5. Review your speeches and writings of the past six months. Have you referred to the values of the school?

6. Develop slogans and metaphors to communicate the values of the school.

7. Outline what and how you have monitored in the past six months. Do the time and attention you have devoted to monitoring commu-

nicate what you feel is truly important? Remember, attention is all there is.

8. Advise every member of the administrative team to give priority to the identification and recognition of students and staff who are advancing the values of the school.

9. Read Chapter Nine on celebrating success and implement three of the ideas suggested there. Better yet, establish a team to create a plan to celebrate achievement.

10. Develop or purchase an assessment instrument that gives teachers an opportunity to provide you with feedback on your performance. Compare your perceptions of what you are communicating and modeling with the perceptions of your staff.

11. Conduct that meeting you have been putting off with the staff member whose performance has slipped. Remember the advice of Peters and Waterman (1982) to be tough with values but tender with people.

12. Give teachers greater control of the curriculum. Let teams of teachers establish the scope and sequence of content areas, specific outcomes for each course, and methods of assessment. Monitor the results.

13. Identify individuals or small teams of teachers who have particular talents and interests and give them the authority to plan and present an ongoing staff development program.

14. Let teachers work collectively to develop their teaching schedules.

15. Involve teachers in the hiring of new staff members

16. Use teams to solve problems, create new programs, and develop and deliver instructional programs. Start modestly and develop a record of success.

17. Encourage internal competition among individual teachers or teams of teachers by providing them with comparative data on their performance.

18. Interview teachers individually to determine what's working and what's in the way. Work with them to develop plans for removing the barriers to their effectiveness.

19. Arrange your schedule so that you can devote at least 25% of your time to observing classes and discussing instruction with teachers.

20. Read everything you can on effective teaching.

21. Develop expertise in the synergetic supervision process explained in Chapter Seven.

5

The Principal as a Manager of Climate

The ambience of each school differs.
These differences appear to have more
to do with the quality of life and indeed
the quality of education in schools than
do the explicit curriculum and the
methods of teaching.

—John Goodlad,
Pride and Promise: Schools of Excellence for all People

A positive school climate is perhaps
the single most important expression of
educational leadership.

—Scott Thompson
Foreword to *Improving School Climate*

Schools have a certain "feel" to them. An effective school gives the immediate impression that it is "being run" as opposed to "running". There is an air about the school that suggests it has a direction, a point of view, and an orientation. This "feel" or ambience is referred as school climate or school culture and can be defined as the collective set of attitudes, beliefs, and behaviors within a building that make up the group norm. It is quite clear that the climate of a school can have a major impact on school improvement efforts

Discussions of organizational climate often focus primarily on the degree of satisfaction expressed by the members of the organization. However, a school that seeks to improve must be more than just a warm, friendly place. It must concern itself with achievement by establishing high expectations, challenging students and teachers, assessing performance, and holding individuals accountable. Therefore, school climate should be regarded as a measure of both the satisfaction of teachers and students and productivity, which is described in terms of student achievement. Studies have found the following characteristics in schools that are particularly effective with respect to student achievement:

- Teachers have high expectations for student achievement. They are confident of their ability to teach all students and accept their responsibility to do so.
- Instructional time is protected from distractions.
- The school atmosphere is orderly and generally conducive to learning.
- Learning progress is monitored closely.

There is an ecology of high expectations that affects teachers and students alike. Teachers and students recognize that academic achievement is both expected and valued. Instructional time is regarded as too important to waste. Behavior that interferes with the ability of a teacher to teach or a student to learn is not tolerated. Procedures are in place to assess student achievement, and the results are shared with students and faculty. In short, the norms, attitudes, and procedures at work in an effective school reinforce the notion that learning is the central mission of the school.

The research on effective schools consistently has pointed to the principal as the key figure in shaping the climate of a school. Kelley (1980, 53) put it this way:

> If there is a single tool a principal should have, it is a mirror. Looking in that mirror, the principal can find the person who more than any other is both responsible for and accountable for the feelings of satisfaction and productivity for staff, students, and patrons.

Given the tremendous influence of the principal on school climate, a basic issue confronting principals is how to exercise that influence in a positive way.

THE CRITICAL IMPORTANCE OF GOOD DISCIPLINE

According to Abraham Maslow's oft-cited hierarchy of needs, people cannot attend to their higher needs until their basic needs have been satisfied. Thus a person's essential physiological needs must be met before he or she will consider such higher needs as security, belonging, esteem, and, ultimately, self-actualization. Applying this analogy to a school, the need for the safety and orderliness that accompany good discipline must be satisfied before the school can address such higher needs as a well-articulated curriculum, instructional effectiveness, teacher empowerment, and, ultimately, sustained educational excellence.

Of all the issues confronting public education in the United States, the issue of greatest concern to the American people has consistently been the lack of student discipline in the schools. In the 1991 Gallup Poll to determine public opinion about the nation's schools, "lack of discipline" and "use of drugs," another issue associated with student behavior, were once again the top two issues, continuing a trend that has lasted more than a decade (Elam, Rose, and Gallup, 1991). A task force on school violence and discipline (Discipline in the Public Schools, 1984, 10) appointed by President Reagan, concluded that "school disorder is among the most significant and perhaps the most overlooked, civil rights issue of the 1980's."

Obviously a school with a reputation for poor discipline will not be regarded as excellent by the community it serves. But public opinion and community perceptions are not the only reasons for a school to examine its practices in the area of student discipline. Virtually every study on effective schools has cited the ability to maintain an orderly atmosphere conducive to learning as a prerequisite to providing an effective school. As the presidential task force (1984, 11) concluded, "If the American education system is to achieve excellence, the problem of disorder in the schools must be addressed." A principal interested in leading a school to excellence simply cannot afford to overlook this critical area of school climate.

Common Pitfalls In School Discipline

A key element in the disciplinary program of any school is the effectiveness with which students are made aware of expectations regarding their behavior. All too often, schools fail to communicate expectations. Some schools provide no guidelines at all, apparently expecting students to learn the standards of appropriate behavior through some sort of osmosis. Other schools bury students in volumes of specific rules and regulations. Authorities in such schools attempt to anticipate every act to which they might object and then enact a rule forbidding it. However, students tend to be devilishly creative in inventing new situations that are not specifically forbidden by the list of do's and don't's, and thus the rulebook of a school that subscribes to this approach seems to be constantly expanding.

A second problem with the approach many schools take to student discipline is that there are no positive incentives for students to remain within the rules of the school. School disciplinary systems are generally built on disincentives or penalties for failure to observe the rules. If a student is willing to risk a short-term consequence such as detentions a parent conference, or a suspension as the price for a certain activity (for example, cutting a class), the school offers no positive inducement to refrain from the activity. As a result, the student can reasonably conclude that his or her best interests are served by violating the rule.

A third problem with the disciplinary programs of many schools is the tendency to treat all students the same way. Schools traditionally have had difficulty in maintaining the appropriate balance between two important but seemingly contradictory goals. On the one hand, school officials seek a degree of control. They believe it is important to regulate both the conduct and the course of study of their students. On the other hand, educators realize the importance of teaching students to act responsibly, something that can be accomplished only when there is an element of choice. Throughout most of the history of public education, schools responded to this dilemma of control versus freedom of choice by emphasizing the former. All students were expected to follow a prescribed curriculum and observe the same rules and procedures. In the 1960's and early 1970's, the emphasis shifted to freedom of choice. Open classrooms in elementary schools and open campuses in high schools suddenly provided all students with the opportunity to determine how they would spend their time, and a proliferation of activities and courses enabled them to choose from a number of alternatives in each subject area.

The flaw in both approaches lies in that all students are treated the same. Schools make no effort to discriminate between those who need structure and control and those who do not. Seniors who have exceeded every expectation of their high school and are only months away from the freedom and responsibility of colleges or careers are dealt with in exactly the same manner as entering freshmen.

Finally, administrators and faculty of some schools fail to acknowledge their responsibility to maintain an orderly atmosphere within their schools. In blaming the students, unsupportive parents, a permissive society, or the court system for student misbehavior, these educators have created a self-fulfilling prophesy that both ensures the continuation of inappropriate behavior and absolves them from the responsibility for correcting it.

Establishing Key Values to Direct Student Conduct

The pitfalls cited above can be overcome if a principal is willing to:

- base the discipline code of the school on a few general guidelines or values
- provide students who abide by those values with increasing privileges as they advance through school
- insist that all staff members assume responsibility for the consistent enforcement of those values
- respond promptly and consistently to students who do not adhere to those values

This positive yet assertive approach to school discipline can help to establish the orderly atmosphere that is a prerequisite for an excellent school.

Few of us can remember pages and pages of specific rules and regulations, but we can keep a few general guidelines in mind. If the disciplinary guidelines of a school are truly meant to be useful in directing the activities of students and teachers, if they are truly meant to become part of and to shape the culture of a school, a concise statement of general values is far superior to an encyclopedia of rules.

In one nationally recognized school, the principal led the faculty in a discussion of the general principles of conduct that all students should be expected to observe. The faculty identified two such principles: 1) student behavior should not infringe on the rights of other students, and 2) student behavior should not infringe on the teacher's ability to teach. Those principles now serve as the foundation for the entire discipline program of the school.

This idea of establishing a few general rules to guide student behavior also can be extended into the classroom. The faculty of one high school decided to develop consistent classroom rules that each teacher could agree to endorse and enforce. All teachers agreed that the following four rules could be applied to any class, and they made a commitment to enforce them.

• Arrive to class on time and be prepared for the work at hand.

• Remain attentive to the task at hand during the full period.

• Be considerate of the rights and feelings of others.

• Respond promptly to the directions of the teacher.

Of course, the development of statements of school values or general classroom rules will be strictly an academic exercise unless steps are taken to ensure that every student is familiar with their content. The statement of values should be the basis for student orientation at the beginning of each school year. In traditional student orientation programs, expectations for student behavior either are not addressed or are presented by the administration in the form of a long list of "thou shalt nots." The positive nature of statements of values and expectations can enable orientation to take on a decidedly different tone. In fact, the orientation of new students can be conducted by student leaders who offer the statements as helpful hints for success rather than as threats.

An even more effective means of ensuring that students are well versed in the school's expectations for behavior is to require students to pass a test demonstrating their knowledge of those expectations. One school requires each incoming student to pass an essay test on its statement of values and withholds privileges until the student is able to do so.

Finally, each teacher should review and emphasize the school's guidelines for student behavior with his or her classes. An entire faculty stressing consistent guidelines for behavior can have a powerful influence on shaping student conduct.

Providing Meaningful Incentives for Good Behavior

Innovative schools have successfully established disciplinary systems that provide students with meaningful incentives for observing the rules of the schools. One such system, particularly well-suited for secondary schools, provides a graduated series of privileges that students can earn only by meeting the academic and behavioral standards established by the school. The steps in this sequence of privileges are as follows:

Freshman Year
- No privileges.
- Students are under the immediate supervision of a teacher every period of the day.
- Students must report to a quiet study hall during any period in which they are not scheduled for a class.
- Students have an abbreviated (25-minute) lunch period.
- Students may not leave the campus at any time during the day.

Sophomore Year
First semester:
- No privileges (same as above).

Second semester:
- Students may be provided with an extended (50-minute) lunch period.

Junior Year
- Students may be provided with an extended lunch period.
- Students may be allowed to leave campus during their lunch period if their parents request this privilege in writing.
- Students may be allowed to determine how they will use their "free" time (that is, those periods in which they are not assigned to a class). Options include using the library, auditing a class, lounging in the student commons or designated area of campus, visiting a teacher, having a snack in the cafeteria, etc. However, students may not leave the campus.
- Students may be allowed to drive to school.

Senior Year

- Students may be provided with an extended lunch period.
- They may be allowed to leave campus during their lunch.
- Students may be allowed to determine how they will use their free time. They are free to leave campus during those periods in which they are not assigned to a class.
- Students may be allowed to drive to school.
- Students may be allowed to determine their schedule of classes. Although they are required to select a minimum number of classes, they can determine the sequencing of their classes and free periods. All other students are assigned classes by the computer.

A key to this system of graduated privileges is that the privileges are not assigned automatically but are reserved for those students who have met the criteria established by the school. Such criteria might include a minimum grade-point average, no unauthorized absences, and no disciplinary referrals for a given grading period. Since this system is intended to provide incentives for good behavior, it should be structured so as to continually offer students additional opportunities to earn privileges. Students who fail to meet the criteria for privileges at the end of one grading period should not be denied the privileges forever, but should have an opportunity to earn them if their grades, attendance, and behavior during the next grading period meet the standard. In other words, the school should not consider a student's cumulative record in awarding privileges, since doing so would make it impossible for students who struggled at the start of a year to earn privileges at any point in the year. By giving students a new opportunity each grading period, the school can continually provide both positive incentives for students who are trying to improve and reinforcement for students who have met the standards.

A second key to this system of graduated privileges is the provision that any privilege may be withdrawn from a student at any time if he or she no longer meets the criteria for receiving privileges. The opportunity to have an extended lunch period, free time, or open campus should be contingent upon the students continuing to meet the standards and expectations of the school. Thus seniors whose grades, attendance, or behavior begin to slip should find themselves back in a supervised study hall with the underclassmen.

This program of awarding and withdrawing student privileges benefits a school in two important ways. First, it provides students with an incentive to observe the rules of the school. Students soon realize that it is in their best personal interest to earn good grades and avoid disciplinary problems. Second, the school is provided with its most effective deterrent to misbehavior. Principals in schools that have adopted this system have found that many students who were unaffected by traditional disciplinary measures were extremely concerned about the prospect of losing a much-valued privilege. Upperclassmen who were nonchalant about detention or suspension viewed even a short-term loss of privileges and banishment to a study hall of underclassmen as a humiliating experience to be avoided at all costs.

One of the assumptions underlying this approach to student discipline is the belief that schools should not treat all students the same way but should discriminate in the amount of freedom they permit students to exercise. The amount of freedom given should be based primarily on the individual student's behavior record. Since freshmen have had no opportunity to demonstrate responsible behavior and generally benefit from considerable structure during their introduction to high school, they should have little or no opportunity to exercise freedom of choice. However, wisdom and maturity are not exclusively a function of age, and the opportunity to assume more responsibility for one's time and decisions should not automatically be conferred on students as they advance through school. To paraphrase Barry Goldwater, the equal treatment of students is no virtue; discrimination in dealing with students is no vice. Every student should have the opportunity to earn whatever privileges the school provides, but only those who meet the school's standards should be awarded those privileges.

Assuming Responsibility for Maintaining Good Discipline

In their staff-development manual titled *Creating Effective Schools* (1982, 176), Wilbur Brookover and his colleagues bemoaned the fact that many educators seem to believe that they can do little to resolve the problem of a lack of student discipline. Brookover listed several "myths" these educators have used to explain why they cannot be expected to maintain an orderly atmosphere in their classrooms and schools:

- Children in general are uncontrollable because of the permissiveness of society.
- Parents are no longer supportive of the school.
- Parents cannot control their own children.
- The courts have tied the hands of the schools in terms of student discipline.
- Teacher training institutions do not prepare teachers to deal with the problem of student discipline.

- Certain students, such as low-achieving students, minority students, or students from a low socioeconomic background, cannot be expected to behave.

Such attitudes are indefensible given what we now know about effective schools and effective teachers. As Brookover (1978) concluded, "Schools and teachers DO make a difference... It is the behavior and techniques used by the school and teachers which are the primary determinants of the level of discipline." The presidential task force (1984, 20) concurred when it concluded that the reason schools had failed to come to grips with discipline problems was "the lack of 'will' of school officials to take action."

It should be obvious that attitudes and beliefs about discipline will play a major role in shaping the climate of a school. Certain attitudes must prevail if a school is to be excellent:

- The entire administration and faculty must believe in their ability to create the disciplinary climate of the school.
- The principal must make it clear that each staff member is to assume responsibility for maintaining discipline, not just in individual classrooms but throughout the entire school.
- Teachers must be familiar with the school's standards of student conduct and work to enforce those standards throughout the building.
- Students must be aware of the school's standards of conduct and, at least at the secondary level, believe that if they observe those standards they will be rewarded with increasing privileges.
- Students must recognize that violating the standards of conduct will result in disciplinary measures that are fair, firm, and, most important, inevitable.

Responding Promptly to Discipline Problems

The principal focused on school improvement must work to instill the values of the school in teachers and students by consistently enforcing standards of conduct. Student challenges to these standards are certain to occur. When they do, it is imperative that school officials neither ignore them nor overreact to them. Ignoring the violation of a rule suggests to students and teachers that the school's espousal of the importance of the rule is insincere; overreacting to a violation increases the likelihood that the student will see the response as a personal attack rather than the safeguarding of a standard of behavior.

The concept of logical consequences described by Rudolf Dreikurs and Loren Grey (1968) can be used to determine an effective response to the inappropriate behavior of a student. This concept calls for school officials to respond to a student who has violated a rule by: 1) confronting the student immediately, 2) explaining the rationale for the rule, 3) reminding the student that in choosing to violate the rule he or she has also chosen the consequence that accompanies the misbehavior, 4) advising the student of the exact consequence that will occur should the student choose to violate the rule again, and 5) encouraging the student to stop the inappropriate behavior and observe the rules of the school. This approach to discipline enables school officials to focus on behavior rather than individual personalities and emphasizes to students that they are responsible for both their behavior and the consequences that result.

Ultimately, the success of this or any other approach to discipline depends on the prompt and consistent response of school officials to misbehavior. Principals must devote whatever energy is necessary to providing a response that is so thorough and consistent that students come to regard disciplinary action as the inevitable consequence of misbehavior. By so doing, they can establish a climate that Ron Edmonds (1979, 22) found was characteristic of effective schools — a climate that is "orderly without being rigid, quiet without being oppressive, and generally conducive to the instructional business at hand." Only when such a climate exists can a principal hope to turn the attention of teachers and students to the higher goals that lead to educational excellence.

FOSTERING COLLABORATION

In his extensive study of schooling practices in the United States, Goodlad (1984) found that teachers rarely had the opportunity to join with their peers in collective endeavors. There were few instances of teachers exchanging ideas or practices, and teachers rarely worked together on school-wide problems. The isolation of teachers is apparent to anyone who has spent time in the classroom; indeed, teaching has been described as the second most private act in which adults engage. This isolation poses a formidable barrier to effective school improvement.

Collaborative work behavior is one of the factors most commonly associated with improving schools (Georgiades, Fuentes, and Snyder, 1983). As Phil Schlecty (1990, 89) concluded, "Those who would lead change in schools must be especially attentive to designing the changes and their implementation in ways that foster collegiality." School leaders must recognize that in improving schools, collaboration is the norm (Leithwood, 1990).

In seeking to create a climate that promotes professional collaboration, school improvement leaders must not mistake congeniality with collegiality. The former suggests people getting along with one another, a condition that is certainly beneficial to any organization. The latter requires more than just pleasant relationships. In truly collaborative schools the professionals talk about teaching and learning; observe each other teach; plan, design, research, and evaluate the curriculum; and teach each other what they know about teaching and learning. In other words, they jointly study their craft and share their findings (Barth, 1991).

The use of small teams provides an excellent vehicle for collaboration. Different studies (Naisbitt and Aburdene, 1985; Deal and Kennedy, 1982; Kanter, 1983) have predicted that the use of the small team will characterize organizations of the future. Kanter (1983) found that the small-team concept already plays a major role in our most innovative companies. An analysis of studies assessing the impact of small collegial support groups for teachers concluded that such collaboration resulted in greater student achievement, more positive interpersonal relationships and cohesion as a staff, increased social support within the faculty, and enhanced self-esteem for the educators (Johnson and Johnson, 1987). Whether called task forces, quality circles, problem-solving groups, or shared-responsibility teams, such vehicles for greater participation are an important part of an innovative school.

There are a number of ways in which the small-team concept could be implemented in schools as a means of promoting collaboration. For example:

1. *By grade level or subject.* All teachers of a particular grade in a building could assume responsibility for carrying out such responsibilities as developing curricular outcomes, assessing student achievement, selecting instructional materials, planning and presenting staff-development programs, participating in peer observation and coaching, developing schedules, and hiring new staff.

2. *By similar teaching assignment.* All teachers of accelerated or remedial students could work to develop or coordinate expectations, materials, assignments, disciplinary consequences, methods of evaluation, and so on.

3. *Interdepartmentally.* All teachers of freshman-level courses in the humanities could work to develop particular themes to be emphasized across departments.

4. *In school-wide task forces.* Small groups of teachers could be formed to consider a particular problem and develop recommendations for resolving it.

5. *By area of professional development.* Teams of teachers could jointly pursue training in a given area of professional development. For example, teachers interested in applying cooperative learning techniques in their classrooms could meet as a team to react to presentations on the topic, develop strategies for using it in the classroom, share related articles, plan peer observation and feedback sessions, and serve as a

support group that discusses and analyzes successes and setbacks in their attempt to use the new technique.

The use of small teams promotes collaboration, helps to build consensus, and allows for the development of the leadership potential of a large number of teachers. Furthermore, it accentuates peer pressure, which has been described as "the single, strongest motivating factor for individuals in this post-industrial era" (Deal and Kennedy, 1982, p. 184). In short, the use of small teams is an excellent means of encouraging the collaboration associated with improving schools.

The factor most critical to the success of the small-group process is the willingness of the principal to give the group both significant responsibilities and the power to fulfill them. If principals recognize their responsibilities to empower teachers, the small-group process can be a significant force in the effort to improve schooling.

FOSTERING EXPERIMENTATION

Another of the findings from the research on improving schools is that such schools encourage experimentation. They have an improvement orientation that encourages and supports efforts to improve through the search for new and better ways (Georgiades, Fuentes, and Snyder, 1983). Schlecty (1990, 42) made a compelling argument for experimentation in schools when he declared that "If schools always do what they have done, they will always get what they have got." It should be self-evident that an improving organization requires people who are willing to change.

Thus, a key to school improvement is persuading individuals to approach their responsibilities from a different perspective and/or to attempt to use new techniques and strategies — in short, to experiment. A willingness to experiment is an important precondition for school improvement. In fact, the autonomy and collaboration that characterize effective organizations are important because they are specifically intended to encourage experimentation.

Roland Barth (1991) described a school in which the professional staff is committed to experimentation as a "community of learners" and expressed the conviction that this concept is fundamental to improving schools. He wrote:

> School need not be a place where there are big people who are learned and little people who are learners. A major responsibility of adults in a community of learners is to actively engage in their own learning, to make their learning visible to youngsters and to other adults alike, to enjoy and celebrate this learning, and to sustain it over time even — especially — when swamped by the demands of others and by their work. (162)

The behavior of the principal can serve as a stimulus or impediment to the creation of a school climate committed to experimentation. Experimentation is unlikely to occur unless principals are willing to serve as a safety net for teachers. Setbacks are bound to occur, and every experiment will not be successful. Principals must help teachers see temporary failure and frustration not as a reason to doubt themselves but as a reason to strengthen their resolve. They must not respond to failed experiments by asking "Who is to blame?" but rather, "What can we learn?"

Furthermore, teachers will be unwilling to experiment if they do not believe in their capacity to influence their classrooms and schools in a positive way. Teachers who believe that their efforts cannot bring about meaningful change, who have lost hope that anything new will make a difference in their effectiveness or satisfaction, will be unlikely to experiment. Conversely, teachers with a strong sense of self-confidence and competence will be those most willing to experiment. Principals who hope to encourage experimentation must make a conscious effort to develop this sense of self-efficacy in the professionals within the school. They must recognize that to help others believe in themselves is one of the most important duties of a principal.

Managing Climate by Keeping in Touch

If principals are to monitor and influence the climate of their schools, they must emulate the successful business executives who establish "a vast network of informal open communications . . . a virtual technology of keeping in touch" (Peters and Waterman, 1982, 121-22). Here are some suggestions for establishing such a network.

Management by Walking About

It is a tribute to the popularity of *In Search of Excellence* that the phrase "management by wandering about" (MBWA) has become something of a cliché. The idea behind MBWA is simple: managers should escape from the confines of the office for a good part of each day to keep in almost constant informal contact with others in the organization. They should be highly visible and close to the action.

The idea of MBWA has its corollary in the research on effective schools, which frequently cites the high visibility of the principal as a characteristic of excellent schools. In fact, in light of the remarkable unanimity of opinion on the importance of MBWA, the infrequency with which it is put into practice is equally remarkable. Even the best-intentioned principals tend to become trapped in the office — bogged down in paper work and day-to-day concerns. Principals committed to school improvement must recognize that they cannot monitor the pulse of the school from the office nor motivate by memorandum. Nor can they leave something as important as MBWA to chance. Principals schedule appointments, meetings, and classroom visits in their daily calendar; why not schedule MBWA? They should block out a time on their calendar each day for their MBWA sorties. The time should be varied so that they do not see the same people every day. Contacts should go beyond exchanging casual greetings to discussing significant issues, sharing information, commending achievement, inviting questions, and responding to rumors. Schools will be well served if principals devote as much time as possible to MBWA each day.

Hold Daily Meetings of the Administrative Team

Meetings of building-level administrators are traditionally held infrequently (weekly or monthly) and conducted according to a formal agenda. In large schools these meetings may be the only times administrators see each other. As a result, minor problems and concerns often are allowed to fester and accumulate; and the regularly scheduled meetings can deteriorate into gripe sessions.

One suburban high school resolved this problem by initiating brief, daily meetings of the administrative team. The principal and department heads meet over coffee each morning for 20 minutes. There is no formal agenda, and any member of the team can raise an issue for discussion. Topics can be continued over several consecutive mornings, but the 20-minute deadline is always observed. The administrators in this school found that the practice of holding daily team meetings — a practice that is also observed by many of the nation's best-run companies — had many positive results. Minor problems and concerns could be resolved almost immediately. The formal weekly meetings became more productive, since they could be reserved for more substantive issues. Most important, the informal daily contact helped to build a sense of the administrators as a team united in purpose and effort. When the principal proposed the idea of daily team meetings, almost every department chairperson objected to the intrusion on his or her time. Today they agree that, as a result of the meetings, their administrative team is functioning more effectively than ever before.

The idea of frequent, informal meetings also can be used effectively in smaller elementary schools. An enterprising principal can establish a schedule of daily meetings to confer with teams of teachers — for example, Monday mornings, the first-grade team; Monday afternoons, the second-grade team; and so on. The key is not format or formality; the key is communication.

Teach

Peters and Waterman (1982) reported that the leaders of America's best-run companies make a concerted effort to stay close not only to employees but also to customers. Thus they periodically serve as sales-people for their companies' products, respond to customers' complaints, assist in production, and so on. These executives find that being close to the customer gives them valuable feedback and new insights. Further-more, their participation in the primary tasks of the organization empha-sizes the importance of those tasks.

This "close to the customer" policy also is advisable for principals. They must have empathy for the concerns of teachers and students, and there is simply no better way to become personally involved in the nitty-gritty of the teacher-student experience than by teaching.

There are several benefits that will accrue to a principal who returns to the classroom:

• *A closer relationship with students.* Particularly in large high schools, students view the principal as a distant and remote figure. He or she is a voice over the public address system, a face at infrequent assemblies, an occasional passerby in the hallway. A return to the classroom provides the principal with an opportunity to establish a deeper, richer relationship with at least a portion of his or her students. This makes the principal seem more approachable to all students.

• *Greater empathy for teachers.* Principals tend to forget the frustration of dealing with an unmotivated student, having instruction interrupted by a message from the attendance office, being obliged to carry out administrative tasks such as distributing passes, or facing the student who needs additional help because she has been on a family vacation for three weeks. Although a return to the classroom may not produce any remedies for teacher frustration, at least principals will develop a better understanding of faculty sentiment.

• *Greater credibility with teachers.* A return to the classroom endows a principal with greater credibility when he or she is evaluating the instruction of teachers. Faculty members who are looking for a reason to dispute or ignore the instructional recommendations of a principal have a tendency to fall back on comments like, "It's been ten years since you were in the classroom; that idea won't work now." Furthermore, if the principal is really good in the classroom, models good teaching, and establishes a reputation as an excellent instructor, his or her recommen-dations for instructional improvement will carry considerably more weight than those of a principal who has not taught a class in a decade.

Practicing principals are almost certain to react to the suggestion that they teach with the response, "Where am I suppose to find the time?" The concern is a real one. Studies of the principalship reveal that the typical principal is already devoting nearly 60 hours to the job each week. Nevertheless, the importance and benefits of a principal's staying in touch with his or her school through teaching cannot be overemphasized. As Sizer (1984) observed, any principal who does not have time for teaching should reassess his or her priorities.

One possible solution to the time crunch is to teach units rather than entire courses. In one high school, the principal teaches a three-week unit each quarter. During this time the regular teacher is released from the class to pursue a project of interest. The principal is responsible for all instructional tasks — developing lesson plans, finding materials, writing tests, sending failure notices, etc. — and it is his job to assign each student a grade for the unit.

Keeping in touch with the climate of a school by such means as MBWA, daily meetings with an administrative or teaching team, and regular stints in the classroom will require considerable energy on the part of the principal. Nevertheless, principals who are committed to promoting a positive climate for school improvement must be prepared to demonstrate this level of vitality

STRATEGIES FOR MANAGING CLIMATE

Following are some strategies we recommend to principals interested in managing climate:

1. Review the daily schedule and weekly calendar. Identify intrusions on classroom time that can be eliminated. Ask teachers to help.

2. Unplug the public address system while classes are in session.

3. Review the distribution of the grades assigned by each teacher. Do any staff members have consistently high failure rates that suggest a failure to accept their responsibility to see to it that students learn? If so, it's time to confront the problem.

4. Schedule yourself for *at least* one hour of MBWA at a different time each day of the week.

5. Practice MBWA in such nonacademic settings, as athletic contests, lunch, dances, etc.

6. Hold brief, informal, no-agenda meetings each day with your administrative team or small teams of teachers.

7. Teach on a regular basis.

8. Identify the key values on which you can build the school discipline code.

9. Require students to pass tests on the discipline code.

10. Turn a good share of your student orientation over to student leaders. Train them to articulate the values of the school.

11. Develop a series of sequential privileges that students can earn by observing the rules of the school. Remove privileges of students who fail to observe the rules.

12. Make certain that teachers are aware of and enforce the school's standards of conduct.

13. Use the logical consequences approach to discipline. Your response to misbehavior must be so consistent that students become convinced that misbehavior will inevitably result in a disciplinary consequence.

14. Keep parents informed of each discipline problem encountered by their children.

15. Develop structures to ensure collaboration on the part of teachers.

16. Work with teachers to develop a peer observation program.

17. Allow teams of teachers to develop proposals for their own staff-development program rather than requiring all teachers to pursue the same program.

18. Develop and participate in faculty study groups whose members explore research on given topics, attempt to apply that research in their classrooms, and share their findings with the rest of the group.

19. Establish an entrepreneurial fund to encourage teacher experimentation. Ask teachers to develop proposals for experiments that will lead to significant school improvement. Use the fund to support those experiments through such means as released time for teachers, new materials, curriculum development projects, surveys, etc. Use a teacher task force to identify those proposals that are most promising.

21. Publicly recognize those teachers who are having a positive impact on the climate of the school through their assistance in maintaining an orderly atmosphere, participation in collaborative efforts, or willingness to experiment.

22. Give public support and encouragement to those who have attempted unsuccessful experiments.

6

Sticking to the Knitting: Developing a Focused Curriculum

*If we know what we want children to
know and be able to do upon
completion of their formal education,
other decisions begin to fall into place.
If we don't know, can't agree or won't
say what the system would be
producing if it were doing the job
right, we will wander around aimlessly
through the policy wilderness for years
to come.*

—Chester Finn,
We Must Take Charge

The curriculum is the most important vehicle a school has for transmitting its core values to students. In fact, curriculum decisions represent the fundamental means of translating the value system of a school into the day-to-day experiences of both teachers and students.

Two critical issues must be considered when the curriculum of a school is assessed. The first is the fit, the congruence between the curriculum and the values of the school. Does the curriculum reflect the values that the school is attempting to promote? The second is the focus, the degree to which the curriculum identifies what is truly significant. Many schools suffer from curriculum overload; they attempt to do so many things that nothing is done well. Peters and Waterman (1982, 293) observed that effective organizations have a clear sense of what they are about and a focus that enables them to stick to the knitting. A school can stick to the knitting only if it has a clearly articulated curriculum that drives daily instruction.

FOCUS, FOCUS, FOCUS

There is a saying among those who sell real estate that the three most important factors to consider when buying property are location, location, and location. The appropriate analogy in the area of curriculum advises that the three most important factors in curriculum improvement are focus, focus, and focus. In fact, perhaps the most important decision that educators can make when attempting to improve their schools is determining what *not* to teach. Much of what students are asked to learn is meaningless, isolated trivia. There is little wonder that "Trivial Pursuit" is such a popular game in America, given the fact that most of the citizenry is a product of the public school curriculum.

One way to check the degree to which the curriculum is being trivialized is to monitor homework assignments. While the research on teaching does demonstrate positive correlations between student achievement and homework, these gains depend on the relevance and significance of the homework assignments (among other factors). For example, an eighth-grade social studies teacher teaching a unit on the Soviet Union assigned students a list of words to define as homework. When the student asked her father if he knew what the word "isba" meant, the father responded that he did not know, but urged his daughter to "look it up in the book." The daughter explained that the teacher had advised students that some of the words could not be found in the text book and that students should find the definitions "on their own." As might be expected, the father next suggested the encyclopedia, but after carefully reading the section on the Soviet Union, both father and daughter were forced to conclude that in the collective wisdom of the editors of the World Book Encyclopedia, "isba" was not a term of sufficient significance to warrant inclusion. The next day, the father went to a university library, examined a foreign language dictionary, and finally discovered that an "isba" is a Russian peasant's hut or log cabin.

The sad fact is, the American public school curriculum is packed with the study of isbas. Time is being wasted in the pursuit of meaningless trivia, and time is a teacher's most precious resource. Increasingly teachers convey their perception that they have less discretionary time as more and more of their workday is dictated by external forces. They confront ever-increasing paperwork and more and more directives about what they must teach. They feel a tremendous amount of pressure to "get it all in." Phillip Schlecty (1990) observed:

> ...[T]eachers, faculties, and principals have and more importantly *feel* that they have little control over the way time is allocated in school. The one commodity that teachers and administrators say that they do not have enough of, even more so than money, is time; time to teach, time to converse, time to think, time to plan, time to talk, even time to go to the restroom or have a cup of coffee....[T]ime is indeed precious in school. (73)

One of the most basic concepts in economics is the concept of opportunity costs — the idea that everything has a cost. For example, what it cost a person to go to the library is all of the things a person is *not* doing while they are at the library. The concept of opportunity cost is a critical concept in curriculum focus. Those who have the responsibility for deciding what students should learn must realize that when students spend time learning one thing, the price they pay for learning that particular content is all the things they did not learn that may have been more significant. A student who expends effort and energy in search of a definition for isba has less opportunity to learn the meaning and significance of the word "perestroika." It is imperative that practitioners recognize that the time students spend in the study of meaningless facts robs them of the time they should be devoting to gaining mastery of knowledge and skills that are truly significant.

The Need for Organized Abandonment

Modern organizations have no procedures for conducting the organized abandonment of anything. It is rather remarkable to think of the numerous mechanisms that are in place at the state, district, and building levels that enable content to be added to the public school curriculum. State legislatures, textbook publishers, commercial test developers, curriculum study committees, and special interest groups all serve as instruments for adding to the list of things boys and girls should know. As a result, the American school curriculum is terribly overloaded. One former state superintendent of schools provided the following list of things American schools are expected to do today:

- teach good nutrition habits
- train students in pulmonary-coronary resuscitation
- give specialized instruction for the hard of hearing, the blind, and the neurologically impaired
- treat the emotionally disturbed
- train the mentally retarded
- teach the gifted
- do eye testing
- give inoculations
- teach first-aid procedures
- provide pregnancy counseling
- assist in disease prevention
- inculcate morals, ethics, and values

- stress the prevention of drug, alcohol, and tobacco abuse
- help students develop political know-how
- develop civic responsibility
- provide sex education
- provide suicide counseling
- maintain birth information and age certification data
- provide instruction in good health care and AIDS prevention
- teach driver education
- promote civil and racial tolerance
- foster integration
- teach the principles of the free-enterprise system
- provide career information
- assist in career planning
- detect and report child abuse
- teach telephone manners and etiquette
- instruct in speed reading
- eradicate head lice
- assist in charity fund raising
- provide vocational training
- build economic awareness
- serve hot lunches and breakfasts
- dispense surplus milk and foodstuffs
- do job placement
- stress bicycle safety and pedestrian safety
- promote physical fitness
- assist with bilingual language development
- counsel delinquents
- foster metric education
- provide transportation
- teach consumer education
- counsel students with problems
- follow due process procedures
- protect student privacy
- provide computer literacy

- teach humaneness and individual responsibility
- eliminate sex discrimination
- assist in bladder control
- develop an appreciation of other countries and cultures
- promote the uses of information
- develop the ability to reason
- build patriotism and loyalty to the ideals of democracy
- promote an understanding of the heritage of our country
- build respect for the dignity and worth of the individual
- develop skills for entry into a specific field
- teach management of money, property, and resources
- provide income tax counseling
- develop curiosity and a thirst for learning
- develop skills in the use of leisure time
- teach technological literacy
- teach pride in work
- build a feeling of self-worth and self-respect
- prepare students to live in global society
- teach reading, writing, and arithmetic

Confronted with a curriculum that is a mile long and one-half inch deep, teachers race to "cover" content with little attention to ensuring student mastery of the knowledge and skills to be acquired. And although there seems to be an endless number of ways to add material to the curriculum, in most school districts there is no formalized mechanism or impetus for removing content from the curriculum (unless it is too controversial). One of the most meaningful steps that can be taken to promote significant school improvement is the development of a process that will identify significant curriculum, eliminate unessential material, and provide time for significant curriculum to be taught. The most pressing need in American curriculum today is focus, focus, focus.

THE CURRICULUM AND SCHOOL IMPROVEMENT: A RESEARCH BASE

As the process of reviewing and improving the curriculum is begun, school officials should familiarize themselves with existing research regarding the instructional program of schools. A review of the studies of effective schooling practices presents consistent findings regarding the importance of a well-planned curriculum that is monitored regularly. A synthesis of this research, compiled by the Northwest Regional Educational Laboratory (1990, 15–16), is presented below. This research provides a helpful framework for school leaders as they begin their instructional improvement efforts.

1. The curriculum is based on clear goals and objectives.

- Learning goals and objectives are clearly defined and displayed; teachers actively use building curriculum resources for instructional planning.
- Clear relationships among learning goals, instructional activities, and student assessments are established and written down.
- Collaborative curriculum-planning and decision-making are typical. Special attention is focused on building good continuity across grade levels and courses; teachers know where they fit in the curriculum.
- Staff, students, and the community know the scope of the curriculum and priorities within it.
- Periodic curriculum alignment and review efforts are conducted to insure congruence with school and district goals.

2. Students are grouped to promote effective instruction.

- In required subjects and courses, students are placed in heterogeneous groups; tracks are avoided; underplacement is avoided
- Instructional aides and classroom grouping techniques are used to help keep the adult/student ratio low, especially during instruction aimed at priority objectives.

3. School time is used for learning.

- School events are scheduled to avoid disruption of learning time.
- Everyone understands time-use priorities; school communications highlight the need for time for learning; procedures are developed to maximize learning time.
- Time-use allocations are established among subjects taught; time-use guidelines are followed by staff.
- The school calendar is organized to provide maximum learning time. Prior to adoption, new instructional programs or school procedures are evaluated according to their potential impact on learning time.
- During the school day, unassigned time and time spent on noninstructional activities are minimal; the school day, classes, and other activities start and end on time.

- Student pullouts from regular classes are minimal, either for academic or nonacademic purposes. The amount of pullout activity is monitored and corrective action taken as necessary to keep things in balance.

- Extra learning time is provided for students who need or want it; students can get extra help outside of regular school hours.

4. Teachers and administrators continually strive to improve instructional effectiveness.

- Throughout the school there is an ongoing concern for improving instructional effectiveness. No one is complacent about student achievement; there is an expectation that educational programs will be changed so that they work better.

- School improvements are directed at clearly defined student achievement and/or social behavior problems; strong agreement is developed within the school concerning the purpose of improvement efforts.

- Priority goals for improvement are set that give focus to planning and implementation. Goals that specify desired changes in achievement or social behavior are known and supported in the school community.

- The full staff is involved in planning for implementation; specific recommendations and guidelines provide the detail needed for good implementation; plans fit the local school context and conditions.

- Implementation is checked carefully and frequently; progress is noted and publicized; activities are modified as necessary to make things work better. Everyone works together to help the improvement effort succeed; staff members discuss implementation and share ideas and approaches.

- Resources are set aside to support improvement activities.

- School improvement efforts are periodically reviewed; progress is noted and the improvement focus is renewed or redirected; successes and new goals are reported.

A SYSTEMATIC APPROACH TO PROGRAM DEVELOPMENT

Although the research on effective schools provides an important base for thinking about curriculum, educators also need a framework for thinking about how to systematically develop curricular programs that have the fit and focus necessary to advance the core values of a school. The strategies and procedures for curriculum development offered here represent a general synthesis of several different approaches to curriculum development. These procedures, which can serve as a framework for developing either a school-wide or a subject-specific curriculum, include the following:

1. Develop a general philosophy that is consistent with the vision and values of the school.

2. Develop goal statements.

3. Develop specific plans for the delivery of the curriculum.

Reaching a Consensus About Philosophy

If a school hopes to provide a curriculum that has the support of key groups within the school community, school officials must take steps to involve these groups in the curriculum development process. The strategies recommended in chapters Two and Three for promoting widespread involvement in the development of vision and values are also well-suited to curriculum development. Teachers, parents, administrators, and representatives of the community should be involved in the earliest, most general discussions of the curriculum. As discussion begins to focus on particular content in individual classrooms, participation in the process should become more narrow, with teachers playing the major role.

Initial discussions should consider basic philosophy. Just as a school benefits from a clearly defined vision statement regarding schooling in general, it also benefits from a widely understood statement of beliefs about what it plans to teach — the specific experiences it plans for students. This, quite simply, is the purpose of a statement of basic educational philosophy.

Many educators tend to dismiss educational philosophy as far too esoteric a subject to have any relevance to the daily concerns of their classrooms. Invite them to participate in a discussion of philosophy and you are quite likely to see their eyes glaze over. Discussions are much more likely to be productive if the issue is framed in terms of basic beliefs and assumptions. Almost anyone with an interest in education welcomes the opportunity to discuss ideas about such topics as the characteristics and needs of children, the expectations of the community for the school, the societal factors that should influence education, the relative importance of particular content or knowledge, and so on. Thus, the process of developing curriculum should begin with the following simple questions:

What Do We Believe About Students Who Will Be Attending Our Schools?

Discussion about the nature of the students should be both general and specific. In initial discussions participants should have the benefit of articles, pamphlets, speakers, films, or filmstrips that can help them to identify the general physical, intellectual, and emotional characteristics of the age group under consideration. Once members have that common background information, they can proceed to discuss their beliefs about the boys and girls who attend their particular school. The group should come to an understanding about the composition of the student body in terms of socio-economic level; the percentage of students working below grade level, particularly in English and math; the percentage who go on to post-secondary education; the percentage enrolled in particular special education programs, and so on. The fundamental objective of these discussions is to develop a genuine and accurate feel for the nature of the students who are to be served by the curriculum the group is setting out to design.

What Are the Expectations of the Community for Our School?

Schools do not operate in a vacuum; they must serve the public. Hence a curriculum-development strategy should include an attempt to ascertain the desires and expectations of the community served by the school.

There are many ways to gather community input about what the school should be doing and what the curricular program should be emphasizing. Some schools have community meetings where the school program is discussed and community desires are made known. For example, a school district in the state of Washington hosts a goal-setting dinner each year. At this dinner, which is open to the public, an evaluation of the goals of the previous year is presented and a discussion is held concerning priorities for the coming year. Goals are discussed, clarified, and assigned priorities.

Involving a cross-section of parents on school committees — especially curriculum committees — is another way to get community input. Some schools plan meetings in the homes of community members in various neighborhoods in order to attract parents who might not come to the school for meetings. This type of meeting is particularly effective for schools whose students are bused from many different neighborhoods. Refreshments can be served to add an informal touch. After refreshments, teachers and parents discuss the school and various aspects of the school program. In such an informal atmosphere, people will often say things they would never have brought up in the more formal setting of the school.

Questionnaires, interviews, and telephone calls are still other ways to get input from the community. Whatever strategies are used, the important point to remember is that community acceptance and support are vital to the success of any school program. If community desires and expectations are ignored or even honestly misunderstood, serious problems are likely to develop in the day-to-day operation of the school.

What Are the Social Influences on the Curriculum?

Although it is important to consider what the local community expects of the school, those who have the responsibility of developing a school curriculum must remember that, ultimately, students will have to function in a larger society. If this fact is not kept in mind, schools run the risk of becoming narrow and provincial. Inattention to society and its trends increases the likelihood that schools will prepare students to operate in a world that simply will not exist. Study and discussion of contemporary life and of the larger society outside the school should be an important part of the goal-setting process.

As was previously noted, school cannot teach everything. Increasingly, various interest groups are vying for space in the curriculum, attempting to influence both what is taught and the manner in which it is taught. Discussions about what to include in the curriculum and with what degree of emphasis should be a major focus of the committees. A study of life in the larger society should play an important part in these decisions.

What Are the Goals of Our Curriculum?

Discussions about the nature of the students, community expectations for the school, and contemporary society outside the school should result in written goal statements that are specific enough to give direction to the school program, yet general enough to allow consensus on the part of the various constituencies that make up the working groups. Writing these goals can be a rather difficult task, since different groups are likely to look at the school from very different perspectives. It is often helpful to have one person write a draft of a position paper that reflects the consensus reached in the working groups. This draft statement then can be duplicated and given to group members for their written comments. After the written comments have been discussed, the procedure is repeated until a document is produced that all members can endorse. The final statement may not reflect the exact opinion of each person who participates, but it should express beliefs and goals that each member of the group can support.

The final goal statements should be presented in the form of short, declarative sentences that are consistent with the statement of philosophy and give direction to the daily program. Normally these statements will be fairly broad and will encompass intellectual development, social and personal development, and physical development—in short, all areas of child growth and development. The statement of curriculum goals developed by a nationally recognized school district after extensive community input is presented below as an example of district-wide goal statements.

Students will be expected to:

1. utilize oral and written English effectively in various communication situations

2. understand fundamental mathematical concepts and processes, as well as their practical applications

3. understand and accept their rights and responsibilities as citizens and participate in civic and social groups

4. explore the major social, environmental, and technological issues and advancements facing the nation and the world

5. develop skills and understandings needed to pursue interests and utilize personal talents

6. investigate career and educational opportunities appropriate to individual abilities and interests

7. understand the importance of maintaining physical and emotional well-being

8. develop decision-making, planning, and resource management skills needed for sound judgments and personal problem-solving

Making the Philosophy and Goal Statements Public

Too often groups work diligently to develop philosophy and goal statements regarding the curriculum, only to see them filed away, never to be used again except for accreditation purposes. Philosophy and goal statements can be of enormous benefit to a school and its principal. First, these statements should be a primary consideration in determining the organization of the school. For example, should the school be organized along the traditional grade levels, or would interdisciplinary teams be more appropriate?

Second, once goal statements have been agreed to, they can serve as the guidelines for future curricular decisions. With interest groups increasingly trying to get their particular programs in the public school curriculum, written philosophy and goal statements can be helpful in establishing criteria for making decisions about adopting new programs. A principal is then in a position to say, "Although I'm sure this is a very fine program, the faculty and parents at this school have decided that the school should place an emphasis on other goals."

Third, written goal statements provide a basis for program evaluation. Increasing pressures for accountability are making program evaluation more than something talked about in college classrooms and textbooks. A written philosophy and clear, concise goal statements that are reflective of that philosophy are prerequisites for an effective curriculum evaluation process.

How might one go about making the curriculum philosophy and goal statements public? A small, attractive brochure outlining the school curriculum can be produced inexpensively. The brochure should be made available to anyone, but especially to parents who will be sending their children to the school for the first time. The brochure should contain such information as makeup and size of the student body, data on the faculty, the philosophy and goals of the school program, a brief description of the curriculum, and other more mundane facts such as hours of school operation, telephone numbers, and processes to follow in case of an emergency.

Many schools have a framed copy of their curriculum philosophy and goals hanging in the lobby or somewhere near the entrance of the school. Such a display serves as a constant reminder of what the school is trying to accomplish.

Finally, the best way to make curriculum philosophy and goal statements public is to use them. Throughout the year, groups and committees must be encouraged to make their curricular decisions in light of the school's philosophy and goals. By using the goal statements, faculty and students will heighten their awareness of what the school stands for and what is being emphasized in the curriculum.

PLANNING FOR LEARNING: DETERMINING AND SEQUENCING LEARNING EXPECTATIONS

The heart of curriculum development is the identification and sequencing of specific concepts to be taught. One approach to accomplishing this task is to have teachers meet together according to subject area. (Notice that as the curriculum development process proceeds, the involvement of participants becomes more specialized.) The first task facing each group is to reach a consensus about what significant concepts should be taught in each course in a particular subject area.

For example, to determine the concepts to be taught in a middle school math program, a group could first determine the last two concepts taught in the fifth grade of each feeder school. A math teacher from each feeder school could be asked to meet with the middle school math department, or it might be more expedient for a member of the middle school math department to visit each feeder school. Whatever procedure is chosen should then be repeated with the high school teachers in order to identify the first two math concepts taught in the ninth grade. When this task has been completed, the group has identified the first two concepts and last two concepts to be taught in the middle school math program.

The next step is to determine which concepts fall in between the previously identified concepts. One approach is to have a person at the chalkboard write down the concepts that individuals in the groups identify. The ideas should simply be listed rather than evaluated at this stage. After all ideas have been listed, they can be discussed in terms of appropriateness, possible combinations, overlaps, and so forth. After a period of time, a consensus generally develops about which significant concepts students should be expected to master in each subject area. Agreement must then be reached on the sequence in which the concepts should be taught. Although this step is more critical in highly sequential subjects such as mathematics, it should be addressed in each subject area.

During this process, each subject area group should rely on as many resources as possible. The national professional organizations in virtually all subject areas have issued reports on curriculum reform in their fields over the past few years, and these reports should be a central focus of the discussion. Examining a wide variety of textbooks to see which concepts are included and the order in which they are presented is also beneficial. Topics included on nationally normed standardized tests and the National Assessment of Educational Progress also should be considered. Teachers may wish to invite professors or teachers from other schools to offer suggestions.

The final listing of concepts to be included in each course should be general enough to leave teachers with some flexibility. Although it is critical to ensure that a common core curriculum is provided to all students, that curriculum should not be so crammed or tight as to require lock-step instruction that robs teachers of autonomy. Teachers must have some room to operate within the structure of the curriculum.

WRITING EFFECTIVE UNIT PLANS

The final step is to ensure that individual teachers incorporate the identified concepts into their unit plans. A unit plan should be written for each major concept that is to be taught in each subject area. It is important that these plans be written by the team of teachers responsible for teaching the subject. Teachers seldom use unit plans or guides that have been developed by someone else. Furthermore, teachers are far less likely to feel a sense of ownership in materials if they had no part in preparing them.

An appropriate format for the development of these unit plans is one that requires teachers to answer the following four questions about each unit of instruction.

1. *What do I want the students to be able to do as a result of this unit?* To answer this question, teachers should simply list the behaviors that are expected of a student who has successfully completed the unit. This question requires an answer specific enough to force teachers to think in terms of outcomes, but not so specific as to require unreasonable work on the part of teachers. Using clear, common sense terms rather than educa-

tional jargon will help communicate to teachers that unit planning is a practical endeavor that will be useful to them.

2. *How will I determine if the students are ready for this unit?* This question challenges the teacher to determine how he or she will assess students to determine whether they have the prerequisite skills and knowledge to be successful in the unit. Is it possible that students have already mastered the concept, in which case further instruction would constitute an inefficient use of time? Assessment is an important component of planning and presenting instruction at the appropriate level of difficulty. It may take many forms,such as a written test, a review of student homework, an evaluation of the test results from the previous unit, teacher observation of the students, or question-and-answer sessions. Whatever method is used, teachers should be able to indicate how they will know the students are ready for this particular unit. Thus this step requires teachers to identify the prerequisite skills for each unit of instruction.

3. *What methods and materials will I use to teach the lesson?* Teachers should have a clear idea of the methods and materials they plan to use in each unit of instruction. The constant modification and adjustment of plans based on student performance, which is the essence of good teaching, presupposes the existence of a basic blueprint of how the unit will be taught. One important consideration in preparing the unit plan is providing the opportunity for student practice. Although teachers should be encouraged to include a variety of instructional methods in their unit plans, every unit plan should provide students with an opportunity to practice the behaviors they will be expected to perform as a result of that particular unit.

4. *How will I know whether the students have learned to do the things I wanted them to be able to do as a result of this unit?* There are a number of ways teachers might check to see whether the students have mastered the behaviors listed in the first step of each unit plan. Observation, written tests, questioning, review of homework, and examination of student projects are all appropriate means of making judgments regarding student progress.

Unit plans need not be lengthy, perhaps a page or two. A copy of each unit plan should be on file with the principal or department chairperson, and periodically the unit plans should be put together in a curriculum guide for each subject area. Most important, each teacher should keep copies of his or her unit plans and use them regularly.

A CASE IN POINT

The public schools of Jackson, Mississippi, have been widely recognized for their accomplishments in school improvement. Although the accomplishments of Jackson's schools cover a broad array of schooling practices, their most notable gains have been in the area of student achievement.

The former superintendent of schools, Robert Fortenberry, was often asked, "Where did you begin? If we want to raise student achievement in our district, what should we make our first priority?" Dr. Fortenberry's answer: "The curriculum." Jackson's public schools spent one school year developing what they call their "common body of knowledge," the list of significant skills and behaviors students are expected to master in each subject area. A booklet outlining these skills is available to parents and students as well as teachers.

The school district also has put a great deal of emphasis on developing a testing program that is aligned with the curriculum. Although teachers are encouraged to teach more than they test, it is expected that teachers will not test what has not been taught.

In short, the tremendous gains in student achievement scores are attributable in large part to an increased focus in the curriculum and the development of a testing program that is congruent with the instructional program.

STRATEGIES FOR IMPROVING CURRICULUM FIT AND FOCUS

Given that the central purpose of schools is to be a place where students learn, what they learn and how well they learn is something that cannot be left to chance. The curriculum should be consistent with, or fit, the vision and values of the school. Furthermore, schools should use the curriculum to establish a focus that enables them to stick to the knitting. Following are some strategies recommended to school leaders interested in assessing the fit and focus of the curriculum of their school.

1. Ask teachers to examine the content of the current curriculum. In each unit of instruction currently being taught, ask them to classify content into one of three categories: essential to know, nice to know, unnecessary. Next, ask them to develop strategies for eliminating the unnecessary and ensuring that the "nice to know" material is addressed only after students have mastered the essential content.

2. Develop a procedure for the systematic elimination of content from the curriculum. Make certain that you have a process in place for "organized abandonment."

3. Review with faculty the findings of research on the curricula of effective schools.

4. Evaluate the curriculum. Is it consistent with the vision and values of the school? Does it help teachers and students focus on the most significant goals of the school?

5. Involve appropriate groups in developing specific curriculum improvement plans, making sure that the plans are consistent with the broader plans for general school improvement.

6. Charge teams of teachers with developing curriculum guides for each subject. For each major topic the guides should include a unit plan detailing intended student outcomes, strategies for determining whether students have the prerequisite skills and knowledge, suggested teaching methods and materials, and strategies for assessing whether or not students have achieved the desired outcome.

7. Develop a systematic plan for assessing the effectiveness of the curriculum. (See Chapter Eight.)

7

Monitoring: Paying Attention to What Is Valued

We will subsequently argue that
leading [a school, a small business, or
a Fortune 100 company] is primarily
paying attention.

—Tom Peters and Nancy Austin
A Passion for Excellence

Monitoring, or paying attention, is a key vehicle for communicating the values of the school. Although school leaders should monitor all aspects of a school's programs, this chapter will focus on two areas that are at the heart of the educational enterprise—teaching and learning.

MONITORING TEACHING

Almost all models of teacher supervision and evaluation begin with the pronouncement that the primary purpose of classroom supervision is the improvement of instruction. However, in most schools a visit from the principal signals an inspection or a rating exercise rather than an effort to improve instruction. Using a checklist or rating scale, the principal may evaluate the teacher as "satisfactory" in classroom management, "excellent" in questioning techniques, "superior" in knowledge of subject matter, and so on. Whether the teacher is rated as superior or satisfactory generally has no bearing on his or her compensation; in most school districts teachers are paid according to an established, lock-step salary schedule. Furthermore, once they have received tenure, they cannot be dismissed as a result of performance unless they are proven to be incompetent. Thus, for many teachers, the only effect of such a rating system is to determine whether or not their performance is minimally satisfactory. The system is, in effect, dichotomous, with "fail" represented by "unsatisfactory" and "pass" by all other rating levels. It is small wonder that teachers tend to regard such a system as either threatening or meaningless.

Many of those who defend the traditional approach to teacher supervision argue that periodic inspections help keep the troops on their toes.

However, unwilling employees cannot be supervised (in the traditional sense) into doing the job right. Those who believe that an annual observation and rating either motivates or helps teachers on a day-to-day basis are deluding themselves.

Another factor that has contributed to the sorry state of teacher supervision is lack of agreement as to what actually constitutes good teaching. Teachers frequently charge that they know more about teaching than the principal who is observing their class. Fortunately for educational leaders who are grappling with the problems of supervision, two recent developments have provided both a knowledge base for analyzing teaching practices and a process for supervising teaching. The knowledge base consists of the research findings on effective teaching discussed in Chapter Eight. The process for supervising teachers is the clinical supervision process.

Toward a Clinical Frame of Reference

The clinical approach to supervision was developed by Morris Cogan (1961, 3) and his colleagues through the Harvard-Newton program in the late 1960's. Some of the basic principles of clinical supervision are as follows:

1. The primary goal of clinical supervision is to improve instruction by observing, analyzing, and ultimately changing the behavior that takes place in the classroom.

2. Clinical supervision requires a face-to-face relationship between the supervisor and the teacher. As Robert Goldhammer (1969, 54) observed, "Clinical supervision is meant to imply supervision up close....In every case the notion of face-to-face contact will be fundamental."

3. A major purpose of this approach to supervision is to help the teacher see, as objectively as possible, what is actually taking place in the classroom. Cogan emphasized that the process is designed to deal with performance, not personality; behavior, not persons.

4. Clinical supervision works best when there is mutual trust between the supervisor and the teacher.

5. Clinical supervision encourages the professional and personal autonomy of the teacher.

A number of different writers have developed supervisory models based on the principles of clinical supervision espoused by Cogan. The model developed by Jerry and Elnor Bellon (1982, 27-29) is one of the more practical and effective of these supervisory models and is currently in use in a number of school districts around the country. The Bellon model, which he refers to as synergetic supervision, is based on the following six assumptions:

- Most people want to improve their performance.
- Objective feedback helps to improve performance.
- Pervasive patterns of teaching can be identified.
- When selected patterns of teaching are changed, instruction can be improved.
- Feedback to improve performance will be most effective when there is mutual trust.
- The primary goal of the supervision process is to improve instruction.

The synergetic supervision process consists of three stages: the pre-observation conference, the observation, and the post-observation conference.

The Pre-Observation Conference

The first step in the synergetic supervision process is a conference between the supervisor (generally the principal) and the teacher. This brief (10 to 15-minute) conference takes place less than 24 hours before the observation. Its purpose is to provide the supervisor with an understanding of the teacher's plans prior to the actual observation. The following points are discussed in the pre-observation conference.

1. *Learning context.* What is the relationship of the current unit of study to the course or program goals?
2. *Learner characteristics.* What are the students like? Are there students with special needs or characteristics?
3. *Learner objectives.* What will students learn as a result of the lesson? (Content Objectives) What will the students be doing during the lesson? (Process Objectives)
4. *Assessment.* What process was used to determine the level of student readiness for the lesson? (Pre-assessment) What process will be used to determine whether or not students have achieved the objective(s)? (Post-assessment)
5. *Instructional strategies and materials.* What resources and teaching techniques will be utilized?
6. *Observer focus.* What should be the major focus of the data collection by the supervisor?

The pre-observation conference is an important part of the supervision process for several reasons. First, it gives the supervisor an opportunity to learn the context of the particular lesson being observed, how it fits into the teacher's broader perspective on the curriculum and the class. The effectiveness of any teaching strategy must be addressed in relation to the objectives of a particular lesson planned for a particular group of students for a particular day.

Second, an effective pre-observation conference enables the supervisor to determine what types of data he or she should collect during the classroom observation in order to assess the effectiveness of the lesson.

Third, the conference provides the supervisor and the teacher with an opportunity to discuss the teacher's short- and long-term instructional plans. This in itself is helpful. Planning is an important element of effective teaching, and the pre-observation conference gives the supervisor a chance to assess the ability of the teacher in this critical area.

Fourth, the pre-observation conference is an excellent means of developing the trust that is a critical factor in effective supervision. Teachers generally appreciate the fact that the observer is making an attempt to understand their instructional plans. The supervisor should refrain from making value judgments or critiquing the teacher during this phase of the process; the conference should be viewed as a meeting of two professionals to discuss instructional goals and methods in a collegial manner. As Bellon and Bellon (1982, 47) concluded, "If the pre-observation conference is properly conducted, the collegial relationship between teachers and administrators can be strengthened."

The Classroom Observation

The second phase of the synergetic supervision process, the classroom observation, allows the supervisor to watch the class and gather objective data relevant to the agreed-on focus. The supervisor is not a passive observer; during the observation he or she writes or charts what the teacher and students are saying and doing. Since it is the responsibility of the observer to collect accurate and useful data, he or she must strive to record what is actually happening in the classroom, not his or her feelings about what is happening.

The Post-Observation Conference

In the post-observation conference, the supervisor and the teacher analyze and discuss the data collected during the class observation. The post-observation conference encompasses four steps:

1. *Lesson reconstruction.* The supervisor and the teacher reconstruct what occurred in the classroom using the data collected and their recollections.

2. *Pattern identification.* The supervisor and the teacher analyze the data to identify patterns or trends.

3. *Pattern assessment.* The supervisor and the teacher discuss whether each pattern was positive (helped to achieve the objective), negative (interfered with the achievement of the objective), or neutral.

4. *Planning for future instruction.* The supervisor and the teacher discuss the benefits of the positive patterns, identify strategies to eliminate negative patterns, and suggest areas of focus for the next observation.

The entire cycle — pre-observation conference, observation, and post-observation conference — is repeated three or four times during the year in order to provide the teacher with feedback on the new instructional strategies being practiced. The effectiveness of the process depends on the ability of the supervisor in three areas:

1. *The ability to collect data during an observation.* A key factor in determining the quality of a post-observation conference is the richness of the data that have been collected. Did the observer have a focus that yielded high-quality data? Was the observer able to collect sufficient data? Collecting data is a skill that can be developed only through practice.

2. *The ability to assess data.* A supervisor cannot help a teacher improve instruction unless the supervisor is a student of good teaching. Although principals cannot hope to become content specialists in all areas, they can become process specialists. An impressive body of research on effective teaching has been developed in the past decade. Those responsible for teacher evaluation must first study that research and then help teachers to learn about it. Principals must serve as the link that unites the worlds of researchers and teachers.

3. *The ability to establish and maintain a trusting relationship with a teacher.* Trust is the oil that makes the supervisory process work. Teachers will be unwilling to assess their teaching if they believe the principal will use that information in a punitive way. In order to develop the trust necessary for the process to be effective, an administrator must consistently demonstrate that he or she is trying to help the teacher improve instruction.

The Benefits of the Synergetic Process

The synergetic supervisory process offers several major advantages over the more traditional approaches of supervision.

1. *It enables teachers to analyze and improve their own instruction.* A school could never hope to achieve excellence if the only time its teachers improved their effectiveness was when they were visited and rated by a supervisor. The synergetic process is designed to train teachers to analyze, adjust, and improve their instruction on an ongoing basis. The post-observation feedback they receive about their teaching enables them to become more conscious of their teaching patterns. Furthermore, the discussion of the effectiveness of patterns is a form of individual staff development that helps the teacher become more aware of the research on effective teaching. Positive teaching strategies are reinforced, and teachers are alerted to tendencies or strategies that may be ineffective. Teachers are then able to use the skills and information that they have acquired through this process to monitor and assess their effectiveness even when the principal is not observing.

2. *It alerts the principal to areas in need of staff development.* The process enables the principal to identify the need for additional training for both individual teachers and the staff as a whole.

3. *It enhances the concept of the principal as both leader and empowerer of teachers.* Once again, a major emphasis of this program is to eliminate the need for teachers to rely on others to assess their effectiveness. As teachers are empowered to assess the impact of their teaching, they become the kind of professionals that will be needed if schools are to be transformed — people willing to assume responsibility, take initiative, and monitor their own work. The principal, in turn, becomes a kind of transformational leader who helps develop and nurture those with whom he or she works. Thus the synergetic process is designed to enable the principal to act as both a strong leader and an empowerer of teachers. As Bellon (1971, 4) wrote:

> The clinical process can be a helpful process for the instructional leader in his effort to improve classroom instruction. However, the ultimate goal should be to help the teacher develop an analytical approach about his own classroom behavior.

An expressed commitment to school improvement is likely to ring hollow unless the principal of the school is willing to pay close attention to what happens in the classroom. Simply put, principals who hope to improve their schools must recognize the need to 1) implement a supervision program designed to improve instruction and 2) devote a significant amount of their time to observing teachers in the classroom.

Differentiated Supervision

While many school districts use some form of the clinical model, clinical supervision is not without detractors. Allan Glatthorn (1990) observed:

> ...too often clinical supervision is offered from a "one-up" vantage point: the supervisor, who knows the answers, is going to help the teacher, who needs to be improved. Such a perspective sees teaching as a craft, not a profession. Even a competent experienced teacher is seen as operating at the level of craft, needing feedback from a supervisor about the specific methods of instruction. (176)

The notion that one form of supervision is appropriate to all teachers is also challenged by David Berliner (1988) who postulates that there are five stages in the journey one takes from novice to expert teacher.

> We begin with the greenhorn, the raw recruit, the novice. Student teachers and many first year teachers may be considered novices. As experience is gained, the novice becomes an advanced beginner....Many second and third year teachers are likely to be in this developmental stage. With further experience, and some motivation to succeed, the advanced beginner becomes a competent performer. It is likely that many third and fourth year teachers, as well as more experienced teachers, are at this level. Perhaps, about the fifth year, a modest number of teachers may move into the proficient stage. Finally, a small number of these will move on to the last stage of development — that of expert teacher. (3)

It is quite clear that teachers have varying degrees of skill in analyzing instructional problems, developing problem-solving strategies, and matching those strategies to specific situations. Teachers with little ability in these areas typically require more specific, concrete directions in terms of problem identification and solution. The clinical approach seems well-suited for this stage of development. Teachers with moderate ability benefit from a more collaborative approach to their professional development, one in which the teacher and principal exchange perceptions about problems, assign priorities to them, and jointly generate possible actions to solve them. Gentle negotiation and give-and-take are the norm at this level of development. Finally, teachers who are skilled in identifying problems, visualizing various strategies, anticipating consequences, and selecting the most appropriate response can flourish with a non-directive approach to their professional development — an approach in which the principal simply serves as a colleague who poses questions to help the teacher clarify goals and provides the encouragement and resources to pursue them. Although the ultimate goal of staff development is to enable all teachers to reach the degree of professionalism represented by reflective, self-directed teachers, individuals at different levels of development will require different supervisory responses to facilitate their growth. The point to be emphasized is that no single format provides the only structure through which the professional development of teachers can be pursued. The most effective approach to promoting the professional development of teachers recognizes the different needs and levels of readiness of individual teachers (Glickman and Gordon, 1987).

A nationally recognized school district offers its veteran teachers who have reached a high level of performance the following alternatives to the traditional process of classroom observations by the principal:

1. *Peer Coaching.* Teachers agree to observe each other's classes and both provide and receive feedback on instruction.

2. *Field-Based Research.* A teacher develops an hypothesis and a research project to test that hypothesis. For example, a teacher might propose the hypothesis that the use of cooperative learning strategies will improve student achievement in United States history. The teacher could then identify a particular period in which to use the strategy as well as the measures of achievement that he or she intends to consider. Findings could be presented in a paper and discussed in a department meeting.

3. *Analysis of a Portfolio of Artifacts.* A teacher maintains a file that includes each lesson plan, handout, quiz, test, and exam in a given semester. Analysis might include congruency between what is taught and what is tested, levels of test questions, etc.

4. *Weekly Journal.* A teacher reflects upon which aspects of instruction worked effectively and which did not and records his or her thoughts each day in a journal.

5. *Seminar Discussion Group.* A group of teachers identifies an instructional topic of interest to read about and discuss. Teachers then attempt to implement the strategies under consideration. Subsequent discussions focus on the success of their efforts, the effectiveness of the strategies, modifications they have found helpful, etc.

6. *Preparing and Presenting a Staff-Development Program.* A teacher with interest and expertise in a particular area of instruction develops and presents a program on the topic to other interested staff members.

7. *Team Teaching with the Principal.* A teacher teams with the principal to teach a unit of two to three weeks in duration. Both share responsibility for developing, presenting, and assessing the unit and identifying its problems and successes.

8. *Submission of an Article for Publication.* A teacher prepares and presents two or three articles on instruction or curriculum for publication in professional journals.

9. *Self-Analysis of Videotapes.* A teacher videotapes three different lessons during the course of the year, analyzes the lessons, and writes an assessment of the effectiveness of each.

10. *Extended Mentoring.* A teacher extends the mentor relationship throughout the school year. The mentoring process includes observing the new teacher at several points throughout the year, providing feedback, being observed by the new teacher, and holding frequent discussions about teaching.

11. *Other.* If a teacher has other ideas that are in keeping with the general objective of promoting serious reflection about teaching, he or she may develop a proposal and discuss it with the principal.

This program not only expands the alternatives available to principals and teachers for promoting professional growth, it also stimulates them to assume the initiative for their own self-renewal. This empowerment increases the likelihood of genuine development. Teacher compliance with practices that are imposed on them is likely to last only as long as an administrator is there to supervise and monitor. Changes that emanate from the experience of teachers are likely to last until the teachers finds a better way.

MONITORING STUDENT ACHIEVEMENT

Chapter Six discussed the importance of developing a curriculum that has widespread support, fits the vision and values of the school, and helps students and teachers to focus on the most significant areas of learning. However, the ultimate measure of the effectiveness of any curriculum is student achievement. Even clearly stated curricular goals will lose their potential to drive the efforts of a school if no effort is made to collect and analyze accurate information about student achievement of those goals. Schools must focus on results rather than activities. However, transforming schools into results-oriented enterprises will occur only if school leaders 1) are able to create measurable indicators of effectiveness in achieving results and 2) constantly apply those measures to analysis. As the research on effective schools has clearly established, the systematic collection and analysis of student achievement data should be a major component of any effort to create an excellent school.

In many school districts the effort to monitor student achievement begins and ends with the administration of a norm-referenced or standardized achievement test. Some districts have abandoned even this limited measure of achievement because of charges that standardized tests are racially biased or are never perfectly matched to the curriculum of the school. Administration of standardized tests certainly should not be the only method of monitoring student achievement. Such tests, however, do provide important information, particularly at the elementary level, and should not be abandoned. If school officials have taken the trouble to analyze different standardized tests to find one that closely matches the curriculum of their school, the results can provide a useful way of comparing the school to national norms. As Ron Edmonds (1982, 14) observed, "Despite all the limitations of standardized tests, I would argue as forcefully as I can that they are, at this moment, the most realistic, accurate and equitable basis for portraying individual pupil progress."

The monitoring of student achievement must go beyond the administration of standardized tests. The basic purpose of standardized tests is to determine how a student compares to a norm group. A school committed to excellence also must concern itself with whether each student has mastered the specific knowledge or skills that the school has identified as objectives. Thus, criterion-referenced tests, in which each item is referenced to a specific learning objective that the student is expected to master, also should be used to monitor student achievement.

The Effective Schools Report (1983) lists the following characteristics of an ideal testing program:

1. Tests are locally developed to ensure that students are tested on what they are actually taught.

2. Tests are nationally normed to ensure that the local definition of mastery is generally congruent with student achievement outside of the district.

3. Tests are curriculum based to emphasize the key concepts of the curriculum to students and teachers.

4. Tests are criterion referenced to provide an assessment of each student in relation to the objectives established by the school.

5. Some tests are standardized to provide a general assessment of the school as it compares to national norms on the content measured.

A CASE IN POINT

Stevenson High School in Lake County, Illinois, used the above guidelines to develop a testing program that the National Center for Exemplary Educational Programs has described as being on the cutting edge of current assessment practices. This small (2,200 students) high school district managed to create and implement an assessment program in which the tests are locally developed, curriculum based, criterion referenced, and, at least in part, nationally normed. It administers nationally normed tests to all sophomores and juniors to provide an analysis of how the achievement levels of its students compare with other students throughout the nation. More than 90% of its students take the ACT exam, and their performance is compared to college-bound students in the nation, the state, and other suburban Chicago high schools. It encourages participation in the Advanced Placement Program of the College Board and uses the results to compare the achievement levels of its top students to other top students across the country. However, the heart of the Stevenson assessment program is its criterion-referenced testing. All teachers identify the specific outcomes that students should be able to achieve as a result of enrollment in the course, and students are provided with a written description of these outcomes. The teachers then develop required, comprehensive final examinations in which each item is referenced to one of the specific course outcomes. Teachers who are assigned to teach the same course coordinate their efforts so as to present identical statements of outcomes as well as identical final examinations. Incorporated within the final examinations are appropriate items culled from released sets of nationally normed examinations such as the National Assessment of Educational Progress. These anchor items give teachers an indication of how the performance of their students compares with that of a national sample.

MAKING EFFORTS TO MONITOR STUDENT ACHIEVEMENT RELEVANT TO TEACHERS

One flaw in the monitoring programs of many districts is the failure to share the results with teachers in any meaningful way. As a result, teachers tend to regard the efforts to monitor student achievement as an administrative function that has little relevance to them. Furthermore, the fact that they do not have the benefit of individual student results means that teachers continue to work in isolation, receiving little or no feedback on the effectiveness of their efforts.

The value of monitoring student achievement arises primarily from its impact on individual classroom teachers. One of the most significant aspects of the Stevenson High School program is that it provides individual teachers with external indicators of their effectiveness. Stevenson uses a computer program to do a thorough analysis of the results of all final examinations. Each examination is subdivided into as many as 15 different subtests. Each teacher is provided with a printout that shows how his or her students performed on each item of the test, each subtest, and on the entire examination in comparison to all other students in the school who completed the exam. The teacher also receives a report on the performance of students who took the test in previous years. Finally, a report on the nationally normed anchor items allows the teacher to see how his or her students performed in comparison to a national sample. Thus teachers are able to compare the performance of their students with that of the current students of their colleagues, past students who completed the course, and students from around the nation. In short, they receive local, longitudinal, and national indicators of their teaching effectiveness.

There are many advantages to this system with its emphasis on coordination of teacher efforts and the provision of meaningful feedback to teachers on the performance of their students. Some of these advantages include:

1. *The system ensures attention to a common curriculum.* If a school truly believes that all students should master certain outcomes, it should take steps to ensure that those outcomes are addressed, regardless of who teaches a particular course. Teachers should play the major role in developing both the student outcomes and the strategies for assessing student mastery of those outcomes. They also should be given the freedom to decide how the outcomes will be addressed on a day-to-day basis. However, it should be made clear to teachers that all students should achieve the outcomes by the end of the course. Common final examinations or other strategies of assessment provide teachers with focus and serve as a check on their attention to the curriculum.

2. *The system results in better tests.* Tests written by a team of teachers are generally superior to those written by individuals because teachers critique one another's questions for relevance, clarity, congruity with outcomes, and so on.

3. *The system promotes teamwork.* Studies of excellent organizations consistently cite the beneficial effects of working together in small teams. Development and analysis of common examinations are a spur to teamwork among teachers of the same course or the same grade level.

4. *The system motivates teachers.* Studies of excellent organizations have concluded that the peer pressure arising from working in teams and the ability to compare one's individual performance with that of others are two of the most powerful motivators. The monitoring program described above is designed to take advantage of both of these motivational strategies.

5. *The system provides teachers with useful feedback on their performance.* Teachers generally work in a vacuum that separates them from other adults and denies them meaningful, objective, results-oriented feedback on their performance. The teacher who has no

idea of how the performance of his or her students compares to that of students in the next room, the next county, the state, or the nation is the norm rather than the exception. Peters and Waterman (1982) stressed that people cannot improve their performance when they work in a vacuum. Individuals need feedback and comparative information to help them assess and enhance their effectiveness. Schools must adopt feedback mechanisms in order to help teachers improve their performance.

Quite often when this approach to curriculum monitoring is presented, the concern is raised that teachers will "teach to the test." But if the test reflects the important, designated outcomes of the course and effectively assesses student mastery of those outcomes, then the test is exactly what teachers should teach to! As Chester Finn (1991) observed:

> ...[T]eaching to the test is a grand thing to do so long as the test does a good job of probing the knowledge and skills one wants children to acquire. If our objectives are sound and our exams carefully aligned with them, we should praise teachers who successfully prepare children for those exams. (162)

Administrators who enthusiastically embrace the idea of analyzing comparative teacher performance as a means of discovering "who the duds are" have missed the point. The practice of providing comparative data to individuals is based on the following assumptions:

1. Most people believe they are good at what they do, but they rely on comparisons with others to assess themselves.

2. If teachers are given objective data demonstrating their effectiveness in comparison to others, they will be motivated to try to improve their performance.

3. Such intrinsic motivation is generally more powerful than a negative evaluation from a supervisor.

If administrators introduce the idea of providing feedback on comparative performance as a means of identifying and weeding out poor teachers, many of the benefits of the program will be lost. Teachers are certain to rebel against a program based on a search-and-destroy mentality; such a program offers little to teachers. On the other hand, a positively orientated, comparative performance program encourages all teachers to consider how they might improve. Given the right climate, a teacher whose students scored above the school average on 14 of the 15 subtests on an examination will feel compelled to try to improve performance on that single deficient subtest. Given the right climate, teachers will turn to one another for ideas on improving performance. Given the right climate, a team of teachers will establish improvement goals and will work to achieve them. The right climate, of course, is one based on trust and respect for teachers as professionals. Certainly administrators should seek to assist teachers whose students are consistently poor performers on examinations; however, the program of providing teachers with comparative performance data should not have the identification of weak teachers as its primary focus.

The results of testing can be reported in a variety of different ways: number of items answered correctly, average standard scores, frequency distributions, and so on. Lorin Anderson (1985, 1-2) argued that the format of reporting student scores that is most useful for making decisions is "percent of students." Anderson explains how that format can be applied to different types of tests:

> For teacher made tests, the percent of students achieving grades of A or B would be presented. For curriculum embedded tests, the percent of students mastering each objective would be presented. For state proficiency/competency tests, the percent of students who meet or exceed the overall standard would be presented. Finally, for nationally normed, commercially produced tests, the percent of students who fall in the highest and lowest national quartiles would be presented.

The percent-of-students format is useful in both establishing and monitoring school improvement plans. For example, the faculty of Stevenson High School used the percent of students scoring at a particular level as the baseline data for each final examination; and then teachers set higher performance standards as part of their goal-setting process. They found that the percent-of-students format provided an excellent means of referencing where the school was, where it wanted to be, and the progress it was making. The percent-of-students format also simplifies the reporting and analysis of data.

Finally, it is important to disaggregate achievement data in a number of ways in order to analyze the effect the instructional program has had on various groups of students. For example, many schools disaggregate their test data by reporting the scores of the students who qualify for free or reduced-price lunches versus those of the students who do not qualify. Some districts also analyze their scores in terms of race or gender.

Toward More Authentic Assessment

A point made in Chapter Six bears emphasis here: Although testing should play a major role in any comprehensive program to monitor student achievement, traditional paper-and-pencil testing is clearly not the most appropriate method of assessment for all of the goals of a school.

Much of what schools are trying to teach — the ability to write, to speak, to create, to demonstrate tolerance, to make responsible decisions — simply cannot be measured by a multiple-choice test. School leaders must work with teachers to identify and develop indicators of student achievement with respect to such goals.

Increasingly, schools are asked to develop alternatives to paper-and-pencil testing that are 1) more "authentic" measures of assessment and 2) consider a broader range of information in evaluating students. Authentic assessment generally requires that students perform a task in a situation that closely matches the challenges of real life. Students are required to demonstrate what they know, can do, or were taught instead of selecting an answer that someone else has written. Their performance is then assessed by a systematic rating procedure. Portfolios of student writing, history projects that require students to act as historians, art work, oral proficiency, and a musical or dramatic performance all can be assessed according to specific criteria for various levels of quality. Diplomas can be presented on the basis of the ability of a student to demonstrate and defend his or her mastery of the core curriculum in public exhibitions rather than on the basis of seat time or Carnegie units. A school interested in a comprehensive program to monitor its curriculum will attempt to incorporate authentic assessment strategies whenever it is feasible to do so.

STRATEGIES FOR MONITORING STUDENT ACHIEVEMENT AND CLASSROOM INSTRUCTION

Monitoring is such a key element in developing excellent schools that it cannot be left to chance. School leaders must monitor all components of the improvement program of a school, but the areas of instructional effectiveness and student achievement merit special attention. The following strategies are recommended to those interested in monitoring these critical areas.

1. Review your procedures for monitoring student achievement in light of the recommendations offered by the *Effective Schools Report* (1983). Do you provide locally developed tests that are curriculum based, criterion referenced, and nationally normed? How closely do the standardized tests you utilize match the curriculum of the school?

2. Ask teachers to develop common measures of assessing student achievement. At the high school level this should include common, comprehensive final examinations that are administered at the end of each course. Grade school teachers should develop and administer common unit assessments following key units of instruction.

3. Review what is done with the data collected as a result of efforts to monitor student achievement. Is the information provided by the testing program used in making decisions about curriculum? Are teachers able to apply the test results to making instructional decisions?

4. Provide each teacher with information regarding the test performance of his or her students compared to that of similar students in the school, in the district, in the state, and in the nation.

5. Accumulate student test data over time so that you can provide teachers with an historical comparison of the performance of their students. Contact Sam Ritchie (Adlai E. Stevenson High School, 16070 W. Highway 22, Prairie View, IL 60069) for information on a computer program that can provide teachers with comparative achievement data.

6. Evaluate the strategies to monitor student achievement in your school according to the criteria of authentic assessment. Do the assessment strategies replicate real-world exercises? Is student performance evaluated according to specified standards? Are students required to demonstrate what they know or can do instead of selecting someone else's answer?

7. Assess your current instructional supervision program. Is its focus clearly on improvement rather than on rating?

8. Read *Classroom Supervision and Instructional Improvement: A Synergetic Process* by Jerry and Elnor Bellon (1982) for a more detailed explanation of the instructional supervision program described in this chapter.

9. Discuss possible changes in the staff-supervision program with the faculty. Try a new supervisory program with a small group of teachers before undertaking a full-scale implementation.

10. Consider the alternatives to traditional teacher observation described in this chapter. Identify three alternatives to try on an experimental basis.

8

Excellence in Teaching

*Even trained and experienced teachers
vary widely in how they organize the
classroom and present instruction.
Specifically, they differ in several
respects: the expectation and
achievement objectives they hold for
themselves, their classes, and
individual students; how they select
and design academic tasks; and how
actively they instruct and communicate
with students about academic tasks.
Those who do these things successfully
produce significantly more
achievement than those who do not,
but doing them successfully demands a
blend of knowledge, energy,
motivation, and communication and
decision-making skills that many
teachers, let alone adults, do not
possess.*

—Jere Brophy and Thomas L. Good
Handbook of Research on Teaching

Central to excellent schooling is excellent teaching. It is impossible to have an excellent school unless the instructional program of the school is characterized by excellence in teaching, and thus it is imperative that principals and teachers become students of effective teaching.

Because teaching is a very complex act, any model of good teaching runs the risk of oversimplification. One model that recognizes this complexity examines teaching effectiveness in three areas: the teacher's content knowledge, technical skills in delivering instruction, and interpersonal qualities. Incorporated in this model is the assumption that each area affects the others and thus improvement in any one area will increase overall effectiveness.

THREE-DIMENSIONAL MODEL OF TEACHING

Content Knowledge

The essence of teaching is the transmission of knowledge to students. Thus one way in which teachers can improve their effectiveness is by improving their knowledge of the subject matter. Efforts to improve instruction generally have been guided by the assumption that teachers have sufficient content expertise and therefore require assistance only in the area of instructional process or delivery. However, it is clear that some teachers present more current and accurate content than others. Excellent teachers continually check their course content (including instructional resources such as films, books, and handouts) to ensure that it is accurate, relevant, and current. They read, take classes, attend workshops, and talk with other teachers. A school can be excellent only if it encourages such self-renewal on the part of teachers and promotes professionalism regarding subject matter.

Once again, organizing teachers into small teams is an excellent means of promoting continued learning. As teachers work together to plan, deliver, and assess instruction, they have an opportunity to evaluate the content of their lessons. The peer pressure associated with teaming is an excellent incentive to ensure both adequacy and accuracy of content.

Technical Skills for Teaching

The majority of findings regarding teaching effectiveness focus on the technical skills of teaching, that is, what effective teachers do when they teach. These findings are not generic in the sense that they apply to each and every situation in the same way. They must be viewed in the context of specific classes, within particular subject areas, and with specific students. If those who use the research on effective teaching keep this caution in mind, they will find that the research provides a useful framework for analyzing personal teaching behaviors and developing instructional improvement efforts. The many studies dealing with instruction present a consistent picture of effective classroom practices. The synthesis of effective teaching research prepared by the Northwest Regional Educational Laboratory (1990) lists the classroom characteristics and practices that are associated with improvements in student performance:

1. Instruction is guided by a preplanned curriculum.

- Learning goals and objectives are developed and prioritized according to district and building guidelines, selected or approved by teachers, sequenced to facilitate student learning, and organized or grouped into units or lessons.

- Unit or lesson objectives are set in a time line so that the calendar can be used for instructional planning.

- Instructional resources and teaching activities are identified, matched to objectives and student developmental levels, and recorded in lesson plans. Alternative resources and activities are identified, especially for priority objectives.

- Resources and teaching activities are reviewed for content and appropriateness and are modified according to experience to increase their effectiveness in helping students learn.

2. Students are carefully oriented to lessons.

- Teachers help students get ready to learn. They explain lesson objectives in simple, everyday language and refer to them throughout lessons to maintain focus.

- Objectives may be posted or handed out to help students keep a sense of direction. Teachers check to see that objectives are understood.

- The relationship of a current lesson to previous study is described. Students are reminded of key concepts or skills previously covered.

- Students are challenged to learn, particularly at the start of difficult lessons. Students know in advance what is expected and are ready to learn.

3. Instruction is clear and focused.

- Lesson activities are previewed; clear written and verbal directions are given; key points and instructions are repeated; student understanding is checked.

- Presentations, such as lectures or demonstrations, are designed to communicate clearly to students; digressions are avoided.

- Students have plenty of opportunity for guided and independent practice with new concepts and skills.

- To check understanding, teachers ask clear questions and make sure all students have a chance to respond.

- Teachers select problems and other academic tasks that are well matched to lesson content so student success rate is high. Set work assignments also provide variety and challenge.

- Homework is assigned that students can complete successfully. It is typically given in small increments and provides additional practice with content covered in class. Work is checked, and students are given quick feedback.

- Parents help keep students involved in learning. Teachers let parents know that homework is important and give them tips on how to help students keep working.

4. *Learning progress is monitored closely.*

- Teachers frequently monitor student learning, both formally and informally.
- Teachers require that students be accountable for their academic work.
- Classroom assessments of student performance match learning objectives. Teachers know and use test development techniques to prepare valid, reliable assessment instruments.
- Routine assessment procedures make checking student progress easier. Students hear results quickly; reports to students are simple and clear to help them understand and correct errors; reports are tied to learning objectives.
- Grading scales and mastery standards are set high to promote excellence.
- Teachers encourage parents to keep track of student progress.

5. *When students do not understand, they are retaught.*

- New material is introduced as quickly as possible at the beginning of the year or course, with a minimum review or reteaching of previous content. Key prerequisite concepts and skills are reviewed thoroughly but quickly.
- Teachers reteach priority lesson content until students show they have learned it.
- Regular, focused reviews of key concepts and skills are used throughout the year to check on and strengthen student retention.

6. *Class time is used for learning.*

- Teachers follow a system of priorities for using class time and allocate time for each subject or lesson. They concentrate on using class time for learning and spend very little time on non-learning activities.
- Teachers set and maintain a brisk pace for instruction that remains consistent with thorough learning. New objectives are introduced as quickly as possible; clean start and stop cues help pace lessons according to specific time targets.
- Students are encouraged to pace themselves. If they do not finish during class, they work on lessons before or after school, during lunch, or at other times so they keep up with what is going on in class.

7. There are smooth, efficient classroom routines.

- Class starts quickly and purposefully; teachers have assignments or activities ready for students when they arrive. Materials and supplies are ready, too.
- Students are required to bring the materials they need to class each day; they use assigned storage space.
- Administrative matters are handled with quick, efficient routines that keep class disruptions to a minimum.
- There are smooth, rapid transitions between activities throughout the day or class.

8. Instructional groups formed in the classroom fit instructional needs.

- When introducing new concepts and skills, whole-group instruction, actively led by the teacher, is preferable.
- Smaller groups are formed within the classroom as needed to make sure all students learn thoroughly. Students are placed according to individual achievement levels; underplacement is avoided.
- Teachers review and adjust groups often, moving students when achievement levels change.

9. Standards for classroom behavior are explicit.

- Teachers let students know that there are high standards for behavior in the classroom.
- Classroom behavior standards are written, taught, and reviewed from the beginning of the year or the start of new courses.
- Rules, discipline procedures, and consequences are planned in advance. Standards are consistent with or identical to the building code of conduct.
- Consistent, equitable discipline is applied for all students. Procedures are carried out quickly and are clearly linked to students' inappropriate behavior.
- Teachers stop disruptions quickly, taking care to avoid disrupting the whole class.
- In disciplinary action, the teacher focuses on the inappropriate behavior, not on the student's personality.

The preceding list of findings should not be translated into a checklist for the evaluation of teachers. The research findings do not constitute a recipe for improving instruction. However, taken together they can provide a broad base for analyzing teaching and creating an awareness among teachers of instructional behaviors that increase the probability of student successes.

Interpersonal Skills of Teaching

Excellent teaching involves more than training students to score well on standardized tests. If we are to have the kind of schools in which teachers are held in high regard by parents and students, the interpersonal aspects of teaching must also be addressed. The research findings regarding the interpersonal skills required for effective teaching are not nearly as strong and consistent as those regarding the more technical aspects of teaching. Nevertheless, an examination of the research on classroom and school climate, effective communication, and personality development reveals a fairly consistent picture of key interpersonal behaviors. This research can be useful as a starting point for discussions with teachers about the interpersonal aspects of excellence in teaching.

Quality of Communication

When we think of improving communication, we tend to think in terms of increasing the quantity of exchanges. However, with both individuals and organizations, it is the quality of communication that is most in need of improvement. This usually involves being a better listener, or as Carl Rogers put it, listening at all levels. If teachers are to be excellent communicators, they must do more than simply transmit subject matter effectively. They must communicate in such a way that students and parents will feel that they have been listened to, that the teacher really cares about them and what they are saying.

Empathy

Excellent teachers remember what it was like to be a student. Helping students become successful is an important aspect of teaching, and it requires a willingness on the part of the teacher to see the student's side. Teacher empathy results in greater sensitivity to the feelings of students. Excellent teachers are careful not only about what they say, but also about how they say it. They are careful about public criticism, and they do not tease or ridicule students. In short, they demonstrate a sensitivity that communicates a sense of understanding and compassion. Empathy does not imply excusing misbehavior; it merely implies realizing that the world of the individual student, parent, or principal may be extraordinarily complex.

Respect

It is important for teachers to model manners and decorum when interacting with students. The difference between the climate created by the teacher who shouts at students to "shut up" and the one created by the teacher who responds to students with consideration and respect is apparent to both an outside observer and to the students in the class. Harshness should never be mistaken for firmness. Teachers can be firm and have high expectations for behavior yet still model respect for students.

Concreteness

Teachers can improve their interpersonal effectiveness by being aware that students need teachers to be specific and concrete. Often teachers encourage students to "do better." Rather than give such abstract directions, teachers should be specific about what students need to do in order to help themselves. Providing frequent, written, concrete guidelines for improvement can be very helpful. They communicate to the student that the teacher has thought carefully about this individual student and what he or she needs to do in order to improve.

Genuineness and Self-Disclosure

Teachers cannot "fake it" when it comes to interpersonal relations with students. Students generally know when teachers are genuine in what they say and do. Genuineness is related, at least in part, to self-disclosure by the teacher. Students are interested in their teachers. They want to know about them and what the are like in the world outside of the classroom. This does not mean that teachers should tell students everything about their personal lives. It merely suggests that students quickly get a feel for the genuineness of a teacher, and this feeling is affected by how much the students get to know the teacher as a person.

Concern

Do teachers care enough about students to confront them when they are harming themselves through their behavior? A black student in a primarily white high school remarked to the assistant principal, "Some teachers don't care enough about us to correct us!" Teachers should correct students if they throw paper down in the halls, if they do work that does not represent their best effort, if they use incorrect grammar, and so on. This is one of the most powerful ways of saying, "I care about you and what happens to you."

Immediacy of Relationship

It is important for teachers to deal with students in the present—today, this week. All too often teachers dwell on the past history of a student in order to explain his or her inadequacies. Teachers also have a tendency to deal too much in the future: "Stay in school and get a good job!" Excellent teachers have a way of dealing with their students in the present. They have an attitude that reflects the notion, "I can't change the past or control the future, but I can teach the students who are in my class today!"

Enthusiasm

Enthusiasm is contagious. Students mirror the enthusiasm of the teacher. It is virtually impossible to get students excited about learning, about discovering new things, and about seeing things in different ways if the teacher does not model enthusiasm. Enthusiasm is demonstrated in many different ways — moving around the room, utilizing a variety of teaching strategies, interacting with students, building on student ideas, and so on. Enthusiasm is more than any one thing teachers do. It is the combination of hundreds of individual behaviors that collectively communicates an attitude of excitement about what the teacher is doing. Ask students to describe the most influential teachers they have ever had, and not one will respond that "he had a great anticipatory set." Invariably, however, they will cite "enthusiasm" when describing their ideal teacher. Enthusiasm is central to developing the positive interpersonal skills needed for excellence in teaching.

Warmth and Humor

Schools need teachers who are warm, caring people. It is impossible, to have an excellent school if teachers are cold, aloof, and indifferent to students. Furthermore, teachers should have a sense of humor — not the ability to tell jokes, but the ability to see humor in situations and to laugh at oneself. Schools are organizations that deal with people, the majority of whom are youngsters. This means that the very best plans are going to go awry from time to time. If teachers do not have a sense of humor, they will be miserable. They will not enjoy the students or teaching, and they will make life miserable not only for themselves but also for those around them. Humor is an important ingredient in creating a positive climate.

Many educators are reluctant to include interpersonal qualities in discussions of effective teaching. There is neither a solid research base nor widespread agreement as to the specific behaviors that constitute positive interpersonal qualities. The importance of a particular interpersonal quality such as warmth is much harder to substantiate than the significance of a technical aspect of teaching such as questioning.

Furthermore, it is much more difficult to effect change in personal behavior than in either content knowledge or specific teaching strategies. Teachers can improve their knowledge of subject matter relatively quickly and easily by reading, attending workshops, and interacting with colleagues. These means also can be used to improve the technical skills of teaching if the element of practice is added. Improving interpersonal skills is a much more amorphous process and usually is accomplished only in small increments over an extended period of time.

Nevertheless, any consideration of excellent teaching must include the interpersonal element. There is a tendency among researchers to measure that which is easiest to measure, but the fact that something is difficult to measure does not negate its importance or suggest that it should be ignored. Teachers and administrators should discuss the interpersonal aspects of teaching and reach some consensus as to how this important area of teaching fits into the school's vision of excellence.

THE TEACHER AS LEADER

The way in which the role of an individual is defined within an enterprise will determine the way that individual goes about his or her job within the enterprise. The role of teachers has been defined in a variety of different ways throughout American history. The role that is most consistent with the characteristics described in this chapter and holds the greatest promise for significant school improvement is the concept of the teacher as leader. Before elaborating on that concept, however, it is useful to consider some of the other conceptual approaches to teaching that have been and continue to be in evidence in American education.

THE TEACHER AS CLERGY

In Colonial America and in the early days of the Republic, teachers were expected to transmit religious and cultural values to students. To the Puritans, the primary reason for schools was to teach reading in order to give children access to the Bible. The first Colonial legislation to require schools, "the Old Deluder Satan Act" of 1647, made the religious motive for establishing schools very explicit. The most frequently used school book in colonial New England, *The New England Primer*, provided a catechistic reflection of Puritan ideology, teaching the alphabet with a series of rhymed couplets referenced to the Bible. Teachers often were viewed as an extension of the town's minister and often were required to assist the minister at such religious services as baptisms and funerals.

Following the Revolutionary War, more attention was given to teaching the traditions and democratic principles on which the Republic was based, and the McGuffey Reader with its Protestant morality tales became the standard textbook of the day. However, teachers were still expected to recognize the sacredness of their profession. Early boards of education were as much concerned with the moral competence of the teachers they hired as they were with their instruction in the classroom. Schlecty (1990, 19) summarized this concept of the teacher as clergy: "Teachers may not literally have had to take vows of poverty, chastity, and obedience, but teachers were not well paid (concern about pay was viewed by many to be a sign of weak commitment to the profession) and female teachers signed contracts that precluded marriage and regulated their courting behavior."

THE TEACHER AS FACTORY WORKER

Urbanization, industrialization, and the influx of immigrants in the late nineteenth century lead to a new role for teachers, the teacher as factory worker. According to this concept, teachers were to inspect, sort, and select students as they moved down the educational assembly line. Student achievement was considered a function of their innate ability (or raw material) rather than the effectiveness of the teacher. The uniform curriculum of an earlier era gave way to different curricula and the tracking of students. The function of the school became to determine the aptitude of a student and set him or her on the appropriate educational path — college preparatory, general, or vocational tracks in high school or bluebirds, robins, and sparrows in elementary school. Like the factory model on which it was based, this concept of teaching promoted standardization, efficiency, and tight supervision in a quest for the development of employee-proof procedures and materials. This concept led to a diminished status for teachers. No longer were they doing the work of angels. Now, popular wisdom suggested that "those who can, do; those who can't, teach."

THE TEACHER AS DIAGNOSTICIAN

A third image of the teacher that has emerged in the last half of the twentieth century is the image of teacher as diagnostician. This concept focuses on meeting the individual needs of children by prescribing appropriate treatment. The task of the teacher is to provide diagnostic testing and to design intervention strategies or treatments for students. In fact, the language of teachers of special education and remedial programs borrows heavily from the language of the medical clinic. As Schlecty (1990, 27) wrote in drawing the comparison between special educators and medical clinicians: "words like *diagnosis and prescription* are used often and the term *instrument* seems ever present."

Each of these concepts — the teacher as clergy, the teacher as factory worker, and the teacher as diagnostician is still in evidence in schools today. There are still frequent calls to make the teaching of values the central function of the school, and there are more teachers dismissed for immorality than incompetence. Schools continue to sort and select students through tracking despite research findings that indicate that the practice is harmful to the majority of students. The excellence movement was yet another attempt to teacher-proof schools through the standardization, supervision, and uniform procedures characteristic of the teacher as factory worker. The concept of the teacher as diagnostician grows more prevalent with the expansion of special education programs. Some states now require the development of an individual educational plan for each student not performing at grade level.

However, none of these conceptual images of the teacher will result in the improvement that is needed in schools. If schools are to make significant improvement, teachers and others must be encouraged to define the role of teacher as the "teacher as leader." As the head of the American Federation of Teachers (Shanker, 1985) wrote:

> Students should not be viewed as inanimate objects moving down the educational assembly line. The central analogy that we need for schools is that students are like workers. If students are workers, then teachers have the same jobs that the executive of a company has. How do I get my workers to come here wanting to work and to take an interest in the quality of their work? (312)

What would be the characteristics of individuals who use the teacher as leader as their "central analogy." First, they would know what they want. Just as a leader must have a clear vision of where the organization is going, teachers must have a clear sense of what they want students to accomplish. The main difference between effective and ineffective teachers is that effective teachers know what they want to accomplish and thus are able to monitor themselves more or less continuously. They know the overriding goals of the course and are able to structure a network of relevant content around the few central ideas. They know how each unit of instruction contributes to achieving the overall goal. They know what students should be able to achieve as a result of each day's lesson and can explain how that lesson fits in a larger context. They have a clear view of the attitudes and behaviors they want students to exhibit in their classrooms and can mentally rehearse strategies to bring about the desired results. Like leaders of any enterprise, they recognize that they will be unable to carry out the other tasks associated with leadership unless they are clear on what they want to accomplish.

Second, teachers who operate under the dictates of the teacher as leader are masters of clear and effective communication. They understand and use the technical aspects of instruction that enhance clarity, as described earlier in this chapter. However, the teacher-as-leader concept requires teachers to go beyond technical skills in presenting the message clearly. They know that what they pay attention to or emphasize is a powerful means of communicating to students what is truly significant. Therefore, they give less attention to shallow coverage of a great number of topics and more emphasis to treating fewer topics in greater detail. They understand that the good teacher is recognizable by the many important things that he or she declines to teach. Yet another technique through which teachers as leaders communicate is modeling. They demonstrate their own enthusiasm for their subject, their students, and their teaching. They are characterized by contagious enthusiasm.

Third, teachers who embrace the analogy of the teacher as leader accept their responsibility to motivate others. They recognize that a sense of self-efficacy is the most critical element in human motivation, and they purposefully set out to convince students that they will be successful in the class. They assess students with each new unit of instruction to ensure that students have the prerequisite knowledge and skills to be successful. They teach in small incremental units with frequent checks for understanding. They establish a reasonable, short-term project and vigilantly monitor the progress of each student. They celebrate student success when it occurs and let a student know that his or her achievement has been recognized and appreciated. Like all great leaders, they recognize that helping people to believe in themselves is one of their highest duties.

Finally, those who conform to the image of teacher as leader are persistent. They are tenacious. After just a few weeks of school, teachers and students often enter into silent pacts. When it has become apparent to the teacher that the student has no interest in learning, the teacher begins to ignore the student, sending the subtle message that "I won't bother you if you won't bother me." Those teachers who define their task as leadership will have no part in such capitulation. They refuse to give up on a student and will harass, bribe, plead, and cajole until the student is no longer theirs. They continue to believe in a student even when a student does not believe in himself or herself. They simply never give up.

One of the unspoken problems in American education today is that teachers and administrators have reached a comfort level with a certain rate of student failure. The fact is, teachers often gauge the appropriate rigor of their instruction by the amount of student failure. If all students do well, teachers are more likely to conclude "It must have been too easy" than "The kids and I did a good job." Most teachers would be horrified if 50% of their students failed. They would agonize over those failures and attempt to develop ways to reduce the rate of failure. However, if the failure rate is 10% or 5%, teachers often suffer no disquiet. They are comfortable with this rate of student failure. Those who subscribe to the analogy of teacher as leader are not content with the failure of any student. They work to eliminate failure as an option for students, and they pursue the elusive goal of success for each student with tenacious patience.

DEVELOPING EXCELLENCE IN TEACHING

If one accepts the premise that the excellence of a school is directly related to the quality of instruction that takes place in classrooms, it follows that principals and school leaders should become students of teaching. They should read about teaching, talk about teaching, think about teaching, and model an interest in teaching that will convey the message that quality teaching is central to the school's vision of excellence. Following are some strategies recommended for school leaders interested in modeling this commitment to excellent teaching:

1. Hold workshops with teachers in which the research on teacher effectiveness is presented and discussed.

2. Hold seminars in which teachers can discuss specific aspects of teaching and share teaching techniques.

3. Acting on the belief that every teacher does something exceptionally well, have a teaching fair where teachers put on demonstrations and exhibits about specific activities or resources that work well for them.

4. Provide each teacher with a notebook containing research findings and ideas for effective teaching. Regularly give teachers new articles and research updates to read and add to their notebooks.

5. Encourage teachers to attend workshops, courses, and conferences that will improve their teaching skills.

6. Visit teachers' classrooms frequently so that classroom visits become a way of life in your school. Encourage teachers to visit and observe each other.

7. If possible, have teachers observe classes in other schools.

8. Make excellent teaching a major theme of the school's improvement plan.

9. Develop a teacher improvement/evaluation program that will encourage and help teachers to improve their instructional skills. (See Chapter Seven.)

10. Develop a process that will enable students to provide teachers with feedback regarding various aspects of teaching effectiveness, including the interpersonal aspects.

9

Celebrating the Success of Your School

In the absence of ceremony or ritual,
important values have no impact.

—Terrence Deal and Allan Kennedy
Corporate Cultures (1982, 63)

Every healthy society celebrates its
values.

—John W. Gardner
On Leadership (1990, 17)

A number of studies have concluded that the public receives most of its information regarding schools from students, the media, and the schools themselves. For a number of reasons, this news should be of major concern to anyone interested in creating an excellent school.

When the baby-boomers were moving through the public schools in the 1960's, more than half of the adults in the United States had children in school. Today only about one-fourth of the adult population has school-aged children. Thus, fewer people receive information about schools and education on a daily basis. Conversely, more people than ever before rely on the media for information regarding public education. This fact gives educators little reason to rejoice. The national media have consistently painted a bleak picture of public education.

But far worse than the image of schools presented by the media is that generated by schools themselves. Schools are their own worst enemy in terms of adversely affecting public opinion. A few years ago contestants on the popular television quiz show, "Family Feud," were asked to respond to the following questions: "You have just received a call from your child's school. Why has the school called?" The same question had been asked to a hundred members of the show's studio audience. The five responses selected most frequently were:

• He has misbehaved.

• He is failing.

- He is doing poor work or missing assignments.
- He is ill or injured.
- He is truant.

This sampling suggests that the most neutral statement parents could hope to hear from a school was that their child was sick. Educators bombard parents with negative messages and then are puzzled when parents react negatively to the schools.

The tendency of educators to stress problems or failures when communicating with the public stands in marked contrast to the practices of the nation's most successful businesses. In their study of America's best-run companies, Peters and Waterman (1982) observed that excellent companies create systems specifically designed not only to produce lots of winners, but also to celebrate winning once it occurs. To satisfy people's desire to be a part of a winning team, these companies continually seek to provide evidence of the success of the organization.

To satisfy the human need to stand out and be recognized for individual ability, they celebrate the efforts and achievements of individuals within the organization. In their analysis of effective business practices, Deal and Kennedy (1982, 60) were emphatic about the importance of celebration to the success of a business organization. They concluded that "a corporate culture, and the values it embodies, must be ritualized and celebrated if it is going to survive."

Schools should heed these messages. There is no evidence to suggest that educators are immune from what Ernst Becker (1973) described as humanity's "essential dualism," the need to feel both a part of a significant collective endeavor and a star in one's own right. Nor is there evidenced to suggest that these yearnings affect only adults. Those interested in spurring a school to excellence should make a systematic and sustained effort to celebrate the success of its teachers and students, both within the school and the larger community.

WORKING WITH THE STAFF

In any organization a sense of success must start from within. Students, parents, and members of the larger community will never develop a high regard for a school unless the staff members within it have that high regard first. Dr. Jerry Bellon (1984), who has consulted in school districts throughout the United States, observed that although he has seen some communities overestimate the quality of their schools and others that do not fully appreciate the job their schools are doing, he has never seen a community that holds its schools in higher regard than the faculty does.

Thus the question becomes, "What can be done to instill a sense of pride among those who work in the school?" Chapters One and Two discussed the importance of drafting a vision statement and communicating values. However, once the vision and guiding values have been identified, it is equally important to reinforce them at every opportunity. Celebrating the evidence of these values is the most effective means of providing such reinforcement. Those interested in promoting school improvement should consider the following recommendations.

Provide Evidence of the School's Success

School leaders must recognize people's innate desire to be on a winning team and continually seek to provide evidence of the school's success. There is much in education that is quantifiable: achievement test scores, passing rates, attendance rates, levels of student participation in extra-curricular activities, grade distributions, survey results, and so on. A concerted effort to monitor, report, and extol the gains that occur in such areas will promote a sense of improvement. Those who dismiss improvements in such areas as insignificant are making a major mistake. The celebrations that surround the delivery record of Frito-Lay employees or the sales achievements of Mary Kay Cosmetics representatives do not just applaud the delivery of corn chips or the sale of makeup. These corporate celebrations promote specific cultural values, establish norms for others to emulate, and convey a sense of the effectiveness of the organization and its people.

Effective companies use celebrations to promote the attitude "we will succeed because we are special." As that attitude becomes pervasive in an organization, it ultimately is recognized by those outside of the organization as well. Deal and Kennedy (1982) illustrated this point with the example of the sales representative who says, "I'm with IBM" rather than "I peddle typewriters for a living." Because of the outstanding reputation that IBM enjoys, the simple statement, "I'm with IBM," serves as a source of personal satisfaction for the sales representative. Furthermore, it heightens his or her expectations for personal performance. Deal and Kennedy concluded that the attitude "we will succeed because we are special" can be maintained only by continually celebrating achievements that reflect the values of the organization. Those interested in promoting particular values within a school must always be on the lookout for indicators of the presence of those values. Teachers must be given evidence that their efforts are having an impact.

Establish a Reward Structure

There is a tendency on the part of those interested in creating excellent schools to establish exceptionally high standards in order to demonstrate the school's commitment to excellence. (Generally those high standards are set by one group for achievement by another: administrators for teachers, teachers for students, and so on.) Peters and Waterman (1982) found this same tendency at work in most companies. However, they also found that the effect of this policy was to ensure that the majority of people in the organization failed to achieve the targets and thus failed to benefit from the company reward system. Employees began to think of themselves as losers and, in time, began acting as losers.

Just the reverse was true of the excellent companies that were studied. These companies created reward systems designed to guarantee that most of the people would meet their goals, which were often set by the employees themselves. These companies reinforced the perception of their employees that they were doing well, a perception that psychologists have found to be one of the prime factors in motivation. By providing their employees with an opportunity to be winners, excellent companies capitalize on the fact that we all want to think of ourselves as winners.

There are undoubtedly those who would dismiss this example from the business world as irrelevant to education because of the reliance of schools on public funding. "We would love to offer more rewards for our teachers," they would argue, "but we cannot use public funds for bonuses when we can't afford new textbooks." Such an assertion is understandable, but it misses the point. Excellent organizations find ways to make extraordinary use of nonmonetary incentives. In fact, they tend to utilize small, symbolic rewards rather than large, lucrative ones. Big bonuses often become political and the cause of resentment for those who don't receive them. The small symbolic reward is more effective in serving as a cause for positive celebration.

One nationally recognized school utilizes the presentation of a small plaque to its staff members as one strategy to ensure lots of winners among the faculty. Several plaques are presented by the principal at every staff meeting to individuals who have demonstrated extraordinary effort and achievement. The principal provides a brief explanation of the recipient's accomplishment, and the plaque is presented with a rousing ovation from the staff. Once each year the principal brings long-stemmed roses to a faculty meeting and invites the staff to present a testimonial and a rose to colleagues who have demonstrated the values of the school. Over the past four years nearly 200 plaques and roses have been distributed to the staff. Unlike a "Teacher of the Year" program that results in one winner and an entire faculty of losers, this program gives everyone the chance to be a winner. Those who hope to stimulate the changes necessary to improve schools should develop similar programs to recognize and reward all those who help advance the school toward its vision.

Make Heroes of Staff Members

There are at least three reasons why those interested in improving schools should give priority to making heroes of staff members by publicizing the efforts and achievements that reflect the values of the school.

1. *Recognition improves the morale of those singled out.* Public recognition of exceptional effort is certain to have a positive motivational effect on the recipient of that recognition. In treating someone as a star, we increase the likelihood that the individual will in fact act like a star.

2. *Recognition affects others on the staff.* People tend to assess their own performance not according to some arbitrary standard but in relationship to the performance of others. As Deal and Kennedy (1982, 38) concluded,

> People can't aspire to be "good" or "successful" or "smart" or "productive", no matter how much management encourages them in those directions. They can, however, aspire to be like someone: "He's just an ordinary person but look how successful he is. I can be successful like that too."

By recognizing the performance of individual staff members, administrators provide the remaining staff members with a model and motivate them to engage in similar behavior.

3. *Public recognition reinforces the values of the school.* Recognition serves as a reminder of what is important. As Tom Peters (1987, 370) observed, "Among other things, well-constructed recognition settings provide the single most important opportunity to parade and enforce the specific kinds of behavior one hopes others will emulate." Recognition is one of the most powerful means available to leaders to demonstrate what is truly valued within the organization.

Here are some specific strategies that can be used in schools to create heroes of staff members.

- Invite parents to write letters of commendation for teachers who have gone above and beyond the call of duty or who have been extremely effective. Ask graduating students to write an essay identifying the teachers who have meant the most to them and why. With the permission of parents and students, periodically publish excerpts from these letters in a newsletter to the staff.

- Establish a program similar to the plaques and roses described previously.

- Devote one section of the school's parent newsletter to a regular feature highlighting faculty accomplishments.

- Send frequent personal letters of commendation and thanks, and place copies of these letters in the teachers' personnel folders. Remember Lee Iacocca's (1984) advice to admonish face to face but praise in writing.

- Publicize the achievement of faculty members through every conceivable means — press releases, newsletters, sign boards, daily announcements, special bulletins, resolutions from the board of education, public award ceremonies, and so on.

- Encourage teachers to share their expertise by making presentations at professional meetings or contributing to professional journals. One district sets aside a special fund to cover the travel expenses of any teacher selected to make a presentation at state, regional, or national conference. Not only is such exposure good for the school, but it is a tremendous means of providing a teacher with a sense of recognition. Administrators in the district also actively support their teachers' proposals for presentations by writing letters of recommendation or endorsement to the professional organization. The same school also publishes its own professional journal composed of articles written by its staff members to encourage teachers to make a contribution to the professional literature and to demonstrate the belief that the school's teachers have ideas worth sharing.

- Watch for opportunities to nominate deserving teachers for awards sponsored by external organizations.

School administrators generally are reluctant to give public recognition to individual teachers. They are concerned that such recognition will be regarded as favoritism or that by recognizing some individuals others will feel slighted, and thus appreciation is expressed surreptitiously (behind closed doors or in private correspondence) if it is expressed at all. Although these concerns are legitimate, they should not prevent a program to make heroes of individual teachers. When the program is initiated, it must be explained that its purpose is to recognize those who are advancing the vision and values of the school; and the entire faculty should be asked to help identify individuals who have done so. Identifying heroes should be the job of everyone in the school, not just the principal. Furthermore, the link between the recognition and the vision and values of the school must be very clear and explicit. Awards and recognition should be presented *only* on the basis of advancing vision and values if they are to serve their intended purpose.

Another issue that those who seek to initiate a recognition program will inevitably confront is at what point does the effort to recognize staff become to much of a good thing. Conventional wisdom suggests that if awards are too frequent they lose their impact, and therefore they should be limited. The practice of placing caps and quotas on awards (no more than five plaques will be presented or no more than 10% of the faculty can be recognized) is contrary to the purpose of a program to promote vision and values through recognition. The only criterion that should be utilized in determining whether or not an award should be presented is the sincerity with which it is given. If the presenter sincerely believes the recipient has advanced the vision and values of the school and feels the award is warranted, it should be presented.

Two points bear re-emphasis. First, in order to be effective, an award program must provide for a wide distribution of awards. A school with only a handful of outstanding teachers will have a difficult time achieving excellence. The reward system should make all teachers feel that they have an opportunity to be recognized and applauded. Second, an achievement need not be monumental to warrant celebration. It is important to vigilantly seek out the small successes — those teachers whose students performed well on a competitive exam or in an extra-curricular contest, who attracted exceptional student enrollment, who modeled their academic discipline by practicing it outside of the classroom, who earned advanced degrees, who were acknowledged as having made a difference in a student life, etc. These teachers merit the recognition of the school community.

Schedule Periodic Social Gatherings for the Staff

Effective organizations use frequent informal gatherings and organizational ceremonies to promote a spirit of oneness and to showcase star performers. Successful organizations also recognize that ceremonies held to welcome new members into the organization or honor members retiring from the organization provide excellent opportunities to promote the values of the organization.

Here are just a few ways in which school leaders can make use of social gatherings to celebrate success.

1. *Develop annual rituals that bring staff members together.* One outstanding school sponsors a series of rituals over the course of the school year. The school year begins with a board-staff dinner for all employees and their spouses. Extra-curricular sponsors are feted later each fall at a beer and bratwurst picnic. A collection among all staff members at the beginning of the year finances monthly after-school parties. Throughout the year the staff enters teams in the school's intramural athletic program, floats in the homecoming parade, and a faculty band in the school variety show. In December, staff members bring their children to school when Santa Claus comes to visit. Faculty teams compete in an annual school wide trivia contest. All staff members are invited to participate in an annual weight-reduction/fitness program that culminates in a party financed by the fines of those who could not meet

their weight-loss goals. In May the principal hosts a party in honor of the teachers who received tenure. There are annual bowl-a-thons, golf outings, and chartered buses to major league baseball games. The year comes to an end with a staff appreciation brunch, at which staff members with perfect attendance and those who have reached a milestone in their seniority (five years, ten years, etc.) are presented awards. Psychologists tell us we all want to feel a sense of belonging, to be a part of the team, one of the "guys." These frequent opportunities to get together reflect a concerted effort to build that sense of belonging.

2. *Provide extensive, ongoing orientation programs for new staff members.* The typical orientation program for new teachers consists of a single day devoted to the explanation of bureaucratic procedures. An orientation program should have the inculcation of the school's values as its primary objective. One school assigns each new teacher a mentor who introduces the individual to the rest of the staff on opening day and presents him or her with the faculty T-shirt. The orientation program continues throughout the year, with administrators and mentors meeting constantly with new staff members to answer questions and reinforce key values. Furthermore, effective orientation programs will not be limited to teachers but also will include secretaries, clerks, custodians, and all of the other employees of the school.

3. *Use retirement as opportunity to demonstrate appreciation for staff.* Effective leaders recognize the adverse effect that an uncelebrated retirement can have on an organization. When someone who has devoted years to an organization is allowed to leave it with little ado, those who remain look upon the organization's lack of appreciation as a sign that their efforts will go unrecognized as well. The school described above turns the retirement of each staff member into a roast complete with amusing speeches, shared memories, and gag gifts. The roast provides an excellent blend of humor and sentiment, but most important it makes a star out of someone who has contributed to the school.

WORKING WITH STUDENTS

The reasons given above for recognizing and celebrating the achievements of staff members apply to students as well. Students too will benefit from the perception that they attend a high quality school and that they are achieving success and recognition. Many of the studies of the effects of positive reinforcement and praise have taken place in the educational setting. Thus it is ironic that educators generally have failed to take advantage of the power of positive reinforcement. The following suggestions are offered as examples of ways schools can celebrate the success of students.

Send Parents Positive Reports on Student Performance

The response of the "Family Feud" audience referred to at the beginning of this chapter provides an indication of how infrequently schools send parents positive messages about the performance of their children. One elementary school addressed this problem by printing a picture of the school on postcards and encouraging teachers to use these cards to let parents know when their students are showing improvement or are doing well. In that community, a picture of the school has thus become associated with good news about children.

A positive approach to progress reports is more difficult to implement in a high school setting, where the student load of individual teachers may run as high as 150 or more. However, software programs are available that enable teachers to send a computer-generated letter simply by circling the name of a student and a number that corresponds to a particular message such as "Just wanted you to know that _____ has been making excellent contributions to class discussion." An administration that makes such a program available to teachers provides a means of getting positive messages to parents and at the same time demonstrates an awareness of teachers' time limitations.

Expand the Practice of Awarding School Letters

If the practice of awarding school letters is designed to both motivate students and build their pride in the school, it seems obvious that schools in search of excellence should seek to expand the opportunities to present such letters. One high school awards letters to all those who participate in athletics rather than limiting the award to those who score a certain number of points or play a minimum number of games. The same school also awards letters to students involved in such extra-curricular activities as drama, choir, band, debate, math team, and school newspaper. Finally, the school presents letters to students who make the high honor roll for the entire year. Walking the halls of this school, one notes that almost all the students are wearing letter jackets; and one can sense the pride these students take in their school.

Increase Honor Roll Recognition

Too often, the only action taken by schools to recognize the students who achieve the honor roll is to issue a press release to the local newspapers. One school that is determined to celebrate the achievements of its students maintains a large scroll that lists the names of all students who made the honor roll in the previous grading period. The scroll is displayed prominently in the main entry area of the school. At the end of each grading period, honor roll students are invited to a continental breakfast with the faculty. Faculty members take full advantage of this opportunity to commend and reinforce the achievement of these students. The principal sends a congratulatory letter to the parents of each honor roll student, and area businesses provide free passes to movies, free hamburgers, an other rewards to these students. At the end of the year, the superintendent hosts a banquet for students who have achieved the high honor roll throughout the year. These efforts have made it clear to the entire school community that this school honors academic performance.

Provide Underclassmen Award Ceremonies

In most high schools the only awards programs to honor academic achievement occur at the end of a student's career at a Senior Awards Night. Students should not have to wait four years to be recognized for their efforts. Annual ceremonies should be held for those underclassmen who have demonstrated extraordinary effort and achievement in a given subject area.

Establish a "Student-of-the-Week" Program

A student-of-the-week program honors students for exceptional service or achievement. A picture of the student is placed on display, along with a narrative describing his or her achievement. Daily announcements call attention to the award. Anyone in the school can nominate a student for this honor.

Turn Your Honors/Awards Ceremony into an Extravaganza

One high school in the suburban Chicago area presents an annual awards ceremony that rivals a Hollywood production. The ceremony is entirely planned and produced by students. Elaborate sets complete with waterfalls, fountains, and curved staircases transform the auditorium stage. A script is written for the entire production. The students who act as masters of ceremony are dressed in tuxedos and long dresses. The school orchestra provides musical interludes as students come forward to accept their awards. Television cameras pan the audience, zooming in on winners as their names are announced. Large-screen televisions placed throughout the auditorium show their reactions to the audience. School officials make no effort to hide the fact that the ceremony is based heavily on the Academy Awards Show. After all, the very purpose of their awards program is to make students feel like stars.

Use Graduation Ceremonies to Honor Student Achievement

Schools often make the mistake of using their graduation ceremonies to focus attention on a valedictorian and a salutatorian to the exclusion of all other students. Such a system is effective in recognizing the students ranked first and second in the graduating class; however, the student ranked third is not even acknowledged. Many schools are now moving to the practice, common in colleges, of having honor-level graduates rather than a valedictorian and salutatorian. Different categories of honors are established, such as highest honors, high honors, and honors. Students in the various categories are then given a distinguishing accoutrement in their caps and gowns, such as a sash, cord, or pin, and are featured in the graduation program. Thus, instead of honoring two graduates, the graduation ceremony can honor the achievements of a significant number of the class members.

Recognize Improvement as Well as Achievement

If schools restrict their recognition to students who are the highest achievers, they ensure that the great majority of students will never receive recognition for their efforts. If the goal is to create as many winners as possible, efforts must be made to celebrate the accomplishments of all students. One elementary school holds bi-monthly assemblies at which each teacher presents awards not only for high achievement, but also for greatest improvement. A high school principal sends congratulatory letters not only to the students who earned the honor roll, but also to those students who showed the greatest improvement over the former grading period. These practices and others like them give recognition to students who are typically overlooked in school awards programs.

Advise Students of the Success of Their School and Their Peers

A school interested in promoting particular values should use every means to publicize the presence of those values, including announcements, press releases, newsletters, special bulletins, signs, display cases, and public ceremonies. Officials should continually advise the school community (particularly the students) of individual and collective achievements that reflect the values of the school.

STRATEGIES FOR CELEBRATING SUCCESS

One important way to further the quest for excellence is to give those within a school a sense that the school is succeeding and that their individual contributions to its success are recognized and appreciated. By celebrating efforts and achievements that reflect the values of the school,

school officials can reinforce the behavior of those who are recognized, provide models for others in the organization, and emphasize what is considered important in that school. The standards for achievement should not be set so high as to make recognition infrequent or exclusive; they should be designed to make stars of as many people as possible. Following are some strategies recommended to school officials interested in celebrating success.

1. Provide evidence of the school's success to those within it. Look for improvements, trends, or accomplishments that can be reported in a positive light.

2. Establish a reward structure that ensures lots of winners. Remember that small symbolic awards are more effective than large ones, which tend to become political.

3. Make heroes of staff members through such means as publishing excerpts from letters of commendation, featuring faculty accomplishments in school newsletters and other available media, sending frequent letters of congratulations and appreciation, providing support (both emotional and financial) to enable teachers to contribute to their professional organizations, and nominating deserving teachers for awards sponsored by external organizations.

4. Use frequent informal gatherings and official ceremonies to promote a sense of belonging and to showcase star performers.

5. Initiate a program to provide parents with positive reports on the performance of their students.

6. Expand the criteria for awarding school letters to include participation in co-curricular activities as well as academic achievement.

7. Increase the recognition given to students who achieve the honor roll by posting their names in the school, sending them and their parents congratulatory letters, hosting a brunch or dinner in their honor, and persuading area businesses to provide them with rewards.

8. Establish a "student-of-the-week" program to honor students for outstanding service or achievement.

9. Turn your honors/awards program into an extravaganza.

10. Develop procedures to ensure that students are recognized for improvement as well as achievement.

11. Increase the number of students recognized at graduation by establishing different categories of honor graduates.

10

Renewal and Persistence: Sustaining the Improvement Process

No organization can maintain
excellence without renewing. No
organization can strive for excellence,
or even attempt to improve, without the
ability to renew.

—Robert Waterman
The Renewal Factor

Nothing in the world can take the place
of persistence. Talent will not; nothing
is more common than unsuccessful
men with great talent. Genius will not;
unrewarded genius is almost a
proverb. Education will not; the world
is full of educated derelicts.
Persistence, determination alone are
omnipotent.

—Calvin Coolidge (1926)

One of the most difficult problems that school practitioners must overcome in their efforts to bring about meaningful school improvement is the mistaken notion that school improvement is a short-term task to be completed rather than a long-term commitment to a new approach. Principals and staffs often have regarded a school improvement initiative as a checklist to complete before going on to other things. As one principal was overheard to say, "last year we did school improvement, this year we are doing cooperative learning." The challenge is how to elicit sustained focus and effort in an enterprise that is notorious for jumping on each passing bandwagon. Practitioners must turn schools into renewing organizations.

A key to the ongoing effectiveness of any organization is its ability to renew itself, to seek and find better ways of fulfilling its mission and responding to change. In some schools, problems may be so obvious that a staff becomes dissatisfied and enthusiastically seeks change. Typically, however, in schools as in most organizations, those within the organization accept things as they are. Innovation is blocked by a thicket of habits, fixed attitudes, settled procedures, and unquestioned assumptions. The conditions found in public education — levels of bureaucracy, the complacency that can accompany tenure, the virtual monopolies within a given geographic area — can accelerate this tendency toward unthinking acceptance of the status quo. The existing way of doing things can rapidly harden into inviolable routines both for individual teachers and an entire school.

This problem can be avoided only if practitioners recognize that one of their most fundamental responsibilities is to help create a school-wide commitment to the continual improvement of teaching and learning. This perpetual disquiet, this constant search for a better way, is the very essence of a renewing organization. The following descriptors of the culture found in renewing organizations developed by Robert Waterman (1987) serve as a useful instrument for analyzing the conditions for renewal within a particular school.

CONDITIONS FOUND IN RENEWING ORGANIZATIONS

1. *Informed Optimism.* Renewing organizations set directions, not detailed strategy. Their primary strategic plan emphasizes flexibility
2. *Direction and Empowerment.* Renewing organizations treat *everyone* as a source of creative input. Their managers define the boundaries and let people decide the best way to do the job within those boundaries. Managers give up a measure of control in order to gain control of what really matters, results.
3. *Friendly Facts, Congenial Controls.* Renewing organizations treat facts as friends. They love comparisons, rankings, measurements, anything that provides context and moves decision-making beyond the realm of mere opinion.
4. *A Different Mirror.* Renewing organizations welcome different perspectives. They listen. They are open, curious, and inquisitive and look for ideas from those outside of the organization.
5. *Teamwork, Trust, Politics, and Power.* Renewing organizations are built on such words as teamwork and trust. They are relentless in breaking down the we-they barriers that paralyze action.
6. *Stability in Motion.* Renewing organizations know how to keep things moving. They attend to the constant interplay between stability and change.

7. *Attitudes and Attention.* Renewing organizations recognize that it is the visible attention of the leadership, not their exhortations, that gets things done.
8. *Causes and Commitment.* Renewing organizations seem to run on causes that get people excited. Commitment results from extensive communication and the ability to turn grand causes into small actions so that people throughout the organization can contribute to a central purpose.

Kanter's (1983) study of companies with a demonstrated capacity to renew also provides useful insight for school practitioners. She found that these companies were characterized by "integrative thinking" that encouraged the treatment of problems as a whole. As she wrote:

> Such organizations reduce rancorous conflict and isolation between organizational units; create mechanisms for exchange of information and new ideas across organizational boundaries; ensure that multiple perspectives will be taken into account in decisions; and provide coherence and direction to the whole organization....Work is done in an environment of mutual respect, participating teams, multiple ties, and relationships that crisscross the organization chart. Furthermore, the large amount of on-the-job socializing that takes place around innovating organizations is not merely an "enlightened fringe benefit"; it serves an important task-related purpose: building a foundation of cross-cutting relationships to make integrative team formation that much easier. (32–33)

Organizations can be growing, learning, and renewing only if those within them recognize the need to examine issues from the perspective of the entire enterprise rather than its fragmented parts (Senge, 1990). Thus the renewing school will break down the barriers that isolate staff, identify the factors that impede the school from its vision, and collaboratively work to address those factors.

THE RENEWING INDIVIDUAL

A major theme of this book has been that people make the difference. Development of an organization that is healthy, vital, and growing depends on individual self-renewal. Renewing organizations are a collection of renewing individuals. In fact, the individual is the source of all organizational renewal (Waterman, 1987). If renewal is to permeate schools and school districts, it is essential that teachers and administrators learn to manage their personal renewal well enough to lead others.

What values must practitioners model to communicate a commitment to renewal? First and foremost, they must not leave their personal self-renewal to chance. As John Gardner (1961) explained,

> Exploration of the full range of his potentialities is not something that the self-renewing man leaves to the chances of life. It is something he pursues systematically, or at least avidly, to the end of his day. He looks forward to an endless and unpredictable dialogue between his potentialities and the claims of life, not only the claims he encounters but the claims he invents. And by potentialities I mean not just skills, but the full range of his capacities for sensing, wondering, learning, understanding, loving and aspiring. (11)

Highly effective individuals work to achieve personal visions by consciously striving to develop their greatest assets " themselves. They constantly seek to establish improvement goals in their physical, spiritual, mental, and emotional lives (Covey, 1989). Schools that encourage staff members to attend to their own self-renewal will enhance the likelihood of becoming renewing schools.

THE IMPORTANCE OF PERSISTENCE

Those who set out on the quest for school excellence must do so with the clear understanding that they can never permit themselves to feel that they have arrived at their destination. The bad news about the pursuit of excellence is that you will never finish. Toynbee's description of civilization also applies to the pursuit of excellence: "it is a movement...and not a condition, a journey and not a destination, a voyage and not a harbor." The renewing school will recognize that this quest for continual improvement is never ending. As efforts to improve in some areas of the school run their courses, efforts to improve in other areas will be initiated; but the effort to improve will never stop.

How can a those interested in school improvement sustain the effort to change when the goal is so elusive and timeless? The answer, the only answer, is persistence. Good ideas and innovations become reality only when they are accompanied by tenacity and courageous patience. People are energized by the vision of an organization only when it is both powerful and persistent. Those who set out to improve a school must realize that organizational renewal is difficult. Setbacks are bound to occur, and every experiment will not prove successful. When Bennis and Nanus (1985), interviewed 90 successful leaders in a wide variety of endeavors, they found that these individuals never used the word "failure" but used such synonyms as "mistake" or "glitch" to describe attempts gone awry. Although they certainly had failures, they viewed them as situations from which they could learn and thus improve the likelihood of success in their subsequent efforts. These men and women attributed their eventual achievement not to charisma or wisdom, but to perseverance. If school improvement efforts are to prevail, principals and teachers must be helped to see temporary failure and frustration not as a reason to doubt themselves, but as a reason to strengthen their resolve.

We hope that this book has offered valuable assistance to those who are willing to work to improve their local schools. It has attempted to offer suggestions as to how they might succeed in that task. However, the most significant factor in determining their eventual success is the ability and courage with which they stay the course. The future of the movement to create new American schools lies not in national reports or state legislatures, but in the effort of those committed to improving their local schools. We wish them well.

STRATEGIES FOR SUSTAINING CHANGE

1. Be persistent.
2. Be persistent.
3. Be persistent.
4. Be persistent.
5. Be persistent.

Appendix:
Developing a Vision Statement

In developing your school's vision statement, it is important to develop a list of characteristics of what constitute an excellent school. One school developed the following detailed description of an excellent school as part of its vision statement. Looking at this list may aid you in developing the vision statement for your own school.

MAINTENANCE OF STANDARDS OF EXCELLENCE

The Board of Education and staff have as a primary goal the maintenance of our school as an excellent school. Both the Board and staff shall be guided in that effort by standards or characteristics agreed to be evident in an excellent school. Those are as follows:

I. PEOPLE

An excellent school is the outgrowth of a Board of Education, administration, staff, parents, students, and community, all of whom share the goal of excellence for that school. In such a school:
1. The staff is characterized by the following (not listed in order of importance):
   a. Professionalism
   b. Motivation
   c. Enthusiasm
   d. Compassion
   e. Creativity
   f. Dedication
   g. Integrity
   h. Morality
2. Staff members possess expertise in their curricular areas and in teaching technique, as well as expertise in their co-curricular and extra-curricular assignments.
3. The faculty is recognized as the heart of the excellent school, and its commitment to excellence is acknowledged by all.
4. The Principal is an active member of the school community and as such provides instructional leadership.
5. Parents play an active role in the education of their children.

6. The Board of Education and its administrative officers facilitate the educational process through informed decision making.
7. Community/parental support for the school is evident by their willingness to serve on advisory committees, booster groups and task forces, by attendance at co-curricular and extracurricular events, by participation at special events, etc.
8. The administrative structure enhances the educational process.

II. RELATIONSHIPS

An excellent school is characterized by an atmosphere of mutual respect and consideration among all members of the school community— students, staff, parents, administrators, Board members, and community members. In such a school:

1. Open communication exists among students, staff, parents, administrators and the Board of Education.
2. Students, staff, and community feel a sense of ownership and pride in the school.
3. The Principal is visible and accessible to students and faculty and, within reason, takes part in the daily activities of the school.
4. Parents and faculty work together to emphasize the value of education and to monitor the academic performance of students.

III. OPPORTUNITIES

Curricular

An excellent school provides all students with an opportunity to pursue a course of study that enables them to become productive and effective citizens. The course of study should expand rather than limit students' choices and opportunities. In such a school:

1. The curriculum clearly reflects the goals of the school, goals that emphasize the nature of the education the school seeks to provide. These goals are understood and accepted by staff, students, and parents and provide a vision of what the school is trying to accomplish.
2. A core of common learning is the essential component of the curriculum. This core comprises the majority of the school's graduation requirements.
3. The core curriculum provides for specialized programs and/or services for students with special needs, abilities and/or interests.

4. The curriculum is geared toward student outcomes, and student advancement through the curriculum and eventual graduation are based upon demonstrated proficiency.

5. There is a systematic attempt to collect information on student achievement and make adjustments to the curriculum on the basis of the results. •

6. There is a constant effort to seek and consider new ways to achieve the school's goals more effectively.

Co-curricular and Extra-curricular

The co-curricular and extra-curricular programs of an excellent school are vital complements to the curricular programs. These programs:

1. directly reflect and enhance the goals of the school

2. are characterized by high levels of student participation

3. result in a sense of community, common interest, and ownership in the school

IV. ATTENTION TO THE INDIVIDUAL STUDENT

Regardless of its size, an excellent school recognizes the value and worth of each individual student. Those within the school make a concerted effort to communicate and demonstrate their concern for each student. In such a school:

1. Attention is paid to facilitating each student's transition to the high school.

2. An effort is made to help each student develop appropriate educational and career goals.

3. The behavior, academic progress, and emotional well-being of each student are continually monitored.

4. Staff members recognize their responsibility to initiate appropriate services to each student.

5. Teachers make every effort to ensure that each student achieves the intended outcomes of their course.

6. Counselors serve as advocates for each student.

7. An effort is made to engage each student in the full life of the school, including its co-curricular program.

8. Each student is provided with the information, assistance, and support to make informed decisions regarding his or her post-graduate plans.

V. EXPECTATIONS

In an excellent school the following expectations are shared by all members of the school community:

Performance

1. Students are expected to invest their best efforts in their academic, co-curricular and extra-curricular pursuits. Teachers accept no less.
2. Teachers present students with specific performance standards for each course or activity.
3. Teachers accept the responsibility to help all students achieve these performance standards.
4. Teachers communicate with parents when performance falls below acceptable standards and offer recommendations and assistance for improvement.

Atmosphere

1. A strong, reasonable behavior code provides clear guidelines for student behavior.
2. The standards of the behavior code are communicated to staff, students, and parents.
3. The behavior code is enforced consistently by the entire staff.
4. There is an effort to help students understand the rationale behind the provisions of the behavior code.
5. The relationships among all members of the school community are characterized by consideration and respect for others.

Recognition of Achievement

1. There is a constant effort to recognize and honor the achievements of the members of the Stevenson school community.
2. There is a constant effort to provide positive reinforcement to students of all ability levels.

V. RESOURCES

An excellent school has sufficient financial resources and facilities to support the academic, co-curricular and extra-curricular programs of the school. We believe that in such a school:

1. There is a constant effort to attract and hold outstanding teachers and administrators.
2. Provisions are made to give staff members the opportunity to stay current in their fields.

3. The maintenance of the building and grounds reflects the pride in the school.

4. Physical facilities are adequate and appropriate; the facilities meet the needs of students and the educational programs of the school.

Bibliography

Alsalam, Nabeel, and Ogle, Laurence, editors. 1990. *The Condition of Education 1990*. National Center for Education Statistics, U.S. Department of Education. Washington, D.C.: U.S. Government Printing Office.

Adler, Mortimer J. 1982. *The Paideia Proposal: An Educational Manifesto*. New York: Macmillan.

American Educational Studies Association. 1985. *Pride and Promise: Schools of Excellence for All the People*. Westbury, NY: American Educational Studies Association.

Anderson, Lorin. 1985. "Frequent Monitoring of Student Progress." Paper presented at South Carolina Conference on Public Schools, Charleston.

Armistead, Lew. 1982. *Building Confidence in Education*. Reston, Va.: National Association of Secondary School Principals.

Barth, Roland. 1990. *Improving Schools from Within*. San Francisco: Josey-Bass.

Becker, Ernst. 1973. *Denial of Death*. New York: Free Press.

Bellon, Jerry. 1971. "Clinical Supervision." Unpublished paper, University of Tennessee.

Bellon, Jerry, and Bellon, Elnor. 1982. *Classroom Supervision and Instructional Improvement: A Synergetic Process*. 2nd ed. Dubuque, Iowa: Kendall-Hunt.

Bellon, Jerry. 1984. "The Teacher as Instructional Leader." Speech presented at Lake County Teachers Institute, Gurnee, Illinois.

Bellon, Jerry. 1988. "The Dimensions of Leadership." *Vocational Education Journal*. November/December. pp. 29–31.

Bennis, Warren, and Nanus, Burt. 1985. *Leaders: The Strategies for Taking Charge*. New York: Harper & Row.

Berliner, David C. 1988. "Implications of Studies of Expertise in Pedogogy for Teacher Education and Evaluation." Unpublished paper, New York.

Berman, Paul, and McLaughlin, Milbrey W. 1975. *Federal Programs Supporting Education and Change, Vol. IV: The Findings in Review*. Santa Monica, CA: Rand Corporation.

Blanchard, Kenneth, and Johnson, Spencer. 1983. *The One-Minute Manager*. New York: Berkley Books.

Blumberg, A., and Greenfield, W. 1980. *The Effective Principal*. Boston: Allyn and Bacon.

Boyer, Ernest. 1983. *High School: A Report on Secondary Education in America*. New York: Harper & Row.

Boyer, Ernest. 1985. "In the Aftermath of Excellence." *Educational Leadership*. March. pp. 10–13.

Brookover, Wilbur, and Lezotte, Lawrence. 1979. *Changes in School Characteristics Coincident with Changes in Student Achievement*. East Lansing: Michigan State University, Institute for Research in Teaching.

Brookover, Wilbur; Beamer, Laurence; Efthim, Helen; Hathaway, Douglas; Lezotte, Lawrence; Miller, Stephen; Passalacqua, Joseph; and Tornatzky, Louis. 1982. *Creating Effective Schools*. Holmes Beach, FL: Learning Publications.

Brophy, Jere. 1979. "Teacher Behavior and Its Effects." Occasional Paper 25, Institute for Research on Teaching, Michigan State University, East Lansing.

Brophy, Jere, and Good, Thomas L. 1986. "Teacher Behavior and Student Achievement." In *Handbook on Research on Teaching.* 3rd ed. Edited by Merlin C. Whittrock. New York: Macmillan.

Brophy, Jere. 1989. "Research: Safe Harbor from Political Winds." *The School Administrator.* January. pp. 25–27.

Burns, James McGregor. 1978. *Leadership.* New York: Harper & Row.

California State Department of Education. 1977. *School Effectiveness Study: The First Year.* Sacramento: California Department of Education, Office of Program Evaluation and Research.

Carlson, Richard O. 1965. "Barriers to Change in Public Schools." In *Change Processes in the Public Schools.* Eugene, OR: Center for the Advanced Study of Educational Administration.

Carnegie Foundation Forum on Education and the Economy. 1986. *A Nation Prepared: Teachers for the 21st Century.* Washington, D.C.: Carnegie Foundation.

Casteen, John. 1985. "The Influence of Leadership, Power, and Authority." In *In Honor of Excellence.* Edited by Marsha Levine. Reston, VA: National Association of Secondary School Principals.

Cawelti, Gordon. 1984. "Behavior Patterns of Effective Principals." *Educational Leadership.* February. p. 3.

Cogan, Morris, L. 1961. *Supervision at the Harvard-Newton Summer School.* Cambridge: Harvard University.

Covey, Stephen. 1989. *The 7 Habits of Highly Effective People.* New York: Fireside Books.

Deal, Terrence, and Kennedy, Allan. 1982. *Corporate Cultures: The Rise and Rituals of Corporate Life.* Reading, MA: Addison-Wesley.

Deal, Terrence, and Peterson, Kent. 1990. *The Principal's Role in Shaping School Culture.* Washington, D.C.: U.S. Department of Education.

DePree, Max. 1987. *Leadership Is an Art.* East Lansing: Michigan State University Press.

Discipline in the Public Schools. 1984. Arlington, VA: Educational Research Service, April.

Dreikurs, Rudolf, and Grey, Loren. 1968. *Logical Consequences: A New Approach to Discipline.* New York: Hawthorn.

Eaker, Robert, and Huffman, James. 1980. Occasional Paper 44, Institute for Research on Teaching, Michigan State University, East Lansing.

Edmonds, Ron. 1979. "Effective Schools for the Urban Poor." *Educational Leadership.* October. pp. 15–23.

Edmonds, Ron. 1982. "On School Improvement: A Conversation with Ron Edmonds." *Educational Leadership.* December. pp. 12–15.

Effective Principal: A Research Summary. 1982. Reston, VA: National Association of Secondary School Principals.

Effective Schools: A Summary of Research. 1983. Arlington, VA: Educational Research Service.

Eisner, Jane. 1979. "Good Schools Have Quality Principals." In *The Journalism Research Fellows Report: What Makes an Effective School*, edited by D. Brundage. Washington, D. C.: Institute for Educational Leadership, George Washington University.

Elam, Stanford; Cramer, Jerome; and Brodinsky, Ben. 1986. *Staff Development: Problems and Solutions*. Arlington, VA: AASA Press.

Elam, Stanley M.; Rose, Lowell C.; and Gallup, Alec M. "The 23rd Annual Gallup Poll of the Public's Attitudes Toward the Public Schools." *Phi Delta Kappan* September pp. 41–56.

Enz, Cathy A. 1986. *Power and Shared Values in the Corporate Culture*. Ann Arbor: University of Michigan Research Press.

Finn, Chester. 1985. "The Dilemmas of Educational Excellence." In *Honor of Excellence*. Edited by Marsha Levine. Reston, VA: National Association of Secondary School Principals.

Finn, Chester. 1991. *We Must Take Charge: Our Schools and Our Future*. New York: Free Press.

Fischler, Abraham. 1971. "Confrontation: Changing Teacher Behavior Through Clinical Supervision." In *Improving In-Service Education: Proposals and Procedures for Change*, edited by Louis J. Rubin. Boston: Allyn and Bacon.

"The Five Correlates of an Effective School." 1983. *Effective School Report* November, p. 4.

Fullan, Michael. 1990. "Staff Development, Innovation and Institutional Development." In *Changing School Culture Through Staff Development*. Edited by Ron Brandt. Alexandria, VA: Association for Staff and Curriculum Development.

Gardner, John. 1961. *Excellence: Can We Be Equal and Excellent Too?* New York: Harper & Row.

Gardner, John. 1983. *Self-Renewal: The Individual and the Innovative Society*. New York: Harper & Row.

Gardner, John. 1990. *On Leadership*. New York: Free Press.

Garfield, Charles. 1986. *Peak Performers: The New Heroes of American Business*. New York: William Morris.

Georgiades, William; Fuentes, Ernestina; and Snyder, Karolyn. 1983. *A Meta-Analysis of Productive School Cultures*. Houston: University of Texas Press.

Glatthorn, Allan A. 1990. *Supervisory Leadership*. Glenview, IL: Scott, Foresman/Little, Brown Higher Education.

Glickman, Carl, and Gordon, Stephen. 1987. "Clarifying Developmental Supervision." *Educational Leadership*. May 64–68.

Goldhammer, Keith, and Becker, George. 1972. *Elementary School Principals and Their Schools*. Eugene, OR: Center for the Advanced Study of Educational Administration.

Goldhammer, Robert. 1969. *Clinical Supervision*. New York: Holt, Rinehart and Winston.

Goodlad, John. 1984. *A Place Called School: Prospects for the Future*. New York: McGraw-Hill.

Herzberg, Frederick. 1966. *Work and the Nature of Men*. New York: World.

Hord, Shirley; Rutherford, William; Huling-Austin, Leslie; and Hall, Gene. 1987. *Taking Charge of Change*. Alexandria, VA: Association for Staff and Curriculum Development.

Hymes, Donald; Chafin, Ann and Gonder, Peggy. 1991. *The Changing Face of Testing and Assessment: Problems and Solutions*. Alexandria, VA: American Association of School Administrators.

Iacocca, Lee, and Novak, William. 1984. *Iacocca: An Autobiography*. New York: Bantam Books.

Johnson, David, and Johnson, Roger. 1987. "Research Shows the Benefits of Adult Cooperation." *Educational Leadership*. November, pp.27–30.

Joyce, Bruce, and Showers, Beverly. 1983. *Power in Staff Development Through Research on Training*. Alexandria, VA: Association of Supervision and Curriculum Development.

Kanter, Rosabeth Moss. 1983. *The Change Masters: Innovation and Entrepreneurship in the American Corporation*. New York. Simon and Schuster.

Kelley, Edgar A. 1980. *Improving School Climate*. Reston, VA: National Association of Secondary School Principals.

Kroc, Ray. 1970. In *Leaders: Strategies for Taking Charge*, by Warren Bennis and Burt Nanus. New York: Harper and Row, 1985.

Leithwood, Kenneth. 1990. "The Principal's Role in Teacher Development." In *Changing School Culture Through Staff Development*. Edited by Ron Brandt. Alexandria, VA: Association for Staf and Curriculum Development.

Levine, Marsha, ed. *In Honor of Excellence*. 1985. Reston, VA: National Association of Secondary School Principals.

Lewis, Anne. 1989. *Restructuring America's Schools*. Arlington, VA: American Association of School Administrators.

Lewis, James, Jr. 1986. *Achieving Excellence in Our Schools . . . by Taking Lessons from America's Best-Run Companies*. Westbury, N.Y.: Wilkerson Publishing.

Lewis, Karen Seashore. 1986. "Reforming Secondary Schools: A Critique and Agenda for Administrators." *Educational Leadership*. September. pp. 33–36.

Lezotte, Lawrence. 1990. *Effective Schools Research Abstracts*. 1990–91 Series. Volume 5, Number 9.

Lieberman, Ann, and Miller, Lynne. 1981. "Synthesis of Research on Improving Schools." *Educational Leadership*. 38 (7) 583–586.

Lipham, James. 1981. *Effective Principal, Effective School*. Reston, VA: National Association of Secondary School Principals.

McLaughlin, Milbrey. 1990. "The Rand Change Agent Study Revisited: Macro Perspectives and Micro Realities." *Educational Researcher*. December, pp.11–16.

Miles, Matthew B. 1965. "Planned Change and Organizational Health." In *Change Processes in the Public Schools*. Eugene, OR: Center for the Advanced Study of Educational Administration.

Naisbitt, John, and Aburdene, Patricia. 1985. *Reinventing the Corporation*. New York: Warner Books.

National Commission on Education. 1983. *A Nation at Risk: The Imperative for Educational Reform*. Washington, D.C.: U.S. Government Printing Office.

National LEADership Network Study Group. 1991. *Developing Leaders for Restructuring Schools: New Habits of Mind and Heart.* Washington, D.C.: Office of Educational Research and Improvement.

Neale, Daniel C.; Bailey, William J.; and Ross, Billy E. 1981. *Strategies for School Improvement.* Boston: Allyn and Bacon.

New York State Department of Education. 1974. *Reading Achievement Related to Educational and Environmental Conditions in 12 New York City Elementary Schools.* Albany: Division of Educational Evaluation.

Norris, B. 1986. "Bennett Foresees a Business Model." *Times Educational Supplement*, August 29, p. 11.

Onward to Excellence: Making Schools More Effective. 1990. Portland, OR: Northwest Regional Educational Laboratory.

Ordovensky, Pat. 1989. "Main Events." *Educational Vital Signs.* Washington, D.C.: National School Board Association.

Peters, Thomas, and Austin, Nancy. 1985. *A Passion for Excellence: The Leadership Difference.* New York: Random House.

Peters, Thomas, and Waterman, Robert, Jr. 1982. *In Search of Excellence: Lessons from America's Best-Run Companies.* New York: Harper & Row.

Peters, Tom. 1987. *Thriving on Chaos.* New York: Harper & Row.

Presidential Task Force on School Violence and Discipline. 1984. Washington, DC: US Government Printing Office.

Process Evaluation: A Comprehensive Study of Outliers. 1978. Baltimore: Center of Educational Research and Development, University of Maryland, February.

Purkey, Stewart, and Smith, Marshall. 1983. "Effective Schools: A Review." *Elementary School Journal.* March. pp. 437–452.

Roberts, Wess. 1987. *Leadership Secrets of Attila The Hun.* New York: Warner Books.

Rogers, Everett. 1962. *Diffusion of Innovations.* New York: Macmillan.

Rosenholtz, Susan, and Simpson, Carl. 1990. "Workplace Conditions and the Rise and Fall of Teachers' Commitment." *Sociology of Education.* October, pp. 241–257.

Rutter, Michael; Maughan, Barbara; Mortimore, Peter; Ouston, Janet; and Smith, Alan. 1979. *Fifteen Thousand Hours: Secondary Schools and Their Effects on Children.* Cambridge: Harvard University Press.

Schlecty, Phillip. 1990. *Schools for the 21st Century: Leadership Imperatives for Educational Reform.* San Francisco: Jossey-Bass.

Selznick, Phillip. 1957. *Leadership in Administration. A Sociological Interpretation.* New York: Harper & Row.

Senge, Peter. 1990. *The Fifth Discipline: The Art and Practice of The Learning Organization.* New York: Doubleday Currency.

Sergiovanni, Thomas. 1967. "Factors Which Affect Satisfaction and Dissatisfaction of Teachers." *Journal of Educational Administration.* pp. 66–82.

Sergiovanni, Thomas. 1984. "Leadership and Excellence in Schooling." *Educational Leadership.* February. pp. 4, 6–13.

Shanker, Albert. 1985. "The Revolution That's Overdue." *Phi Delta Kappan.* 66 (5) 311–315.

Shaw, George Bernard. 1973. *Man and Superman.* Baltimore: Penguin Books.

Showers, Beverly; Joyce, Bruce; and Bennett, Barrie. 1987. "Synthesis of Research on Staff Development: A Framework for Future Study and a State-of-the-Art Analysis." *Educational Leadership*. November, pp.77–87.

Sizer, Theodore. 1984. *A Review and Comment on the National Reports on Education*. Reston, VA: National Association of Secondary School Principals.

Sizer, Theodore. 1985. "The Student-Teacher Triad." In *In Honor of Excellence*. Edited by Marsha Levine. Reston, VA: National Association of Secondary School Principals.

Smith, Wilson. 1973. *Theories of Education in Early America, 1655–1819*. New York: Bobbs-Merrill Company.

Sparks, Dennis. 1984. "Staff Development and School Improvement: An Interview With Ernest Boyer." *Journal of Staff Development*. Fall, pp. 32–39.

Sparks, Georgia Mohlman. 1987. *Promoting The Professional Development of Teachers in Career Ladders*. Oxford, OH: National Staff Development Council.

Taba, Hilda. 1962. *Curriculum Development: Theory and Practice*. New York: Harcourt, Brace and World.

"Teachers Want More Control of the Work Place. . . but only One-Fourth Are Empowered." 1986. *Education U.S.A.*. April 21, p. 4.

Thompson, Scot. 1980. Foreword. *Improving School Climate*. By Edgar A. Kelley. Reston, VA: National Association of Secondary School Principals.

Toynbee, Arnold. 1958. "The Greco-Roman Civilization." *Civilizations on Trial*. London: World Publishing.

United States Department of Education. 1984. *The Nation Responds: Recent Efforts to Improve Education*. Washington, D.C.: U.S. Government Printing Office.

U. S. Department of Education. 1986. *What Works: Research about Teaching and Learning*. Washington, D.C.: U. S. Department of Education.

United States Department of Education, 1991. *America 2000: An Education Strategy*. Washington, D.C.: U.S. Printing Office.

Ventures in Good Schooling: A Cooperative Model for Successful Secondary School. 1986. Reston, VA: National Association of Secondary School Principals.

Waterman, Robert. 1985. In *A Passion for Excellence*. Thomas Peters and Nancy Austin. New York: Random House.

Waterman, Robert H. 1987. *The Renewal Factor*. New York: Bantam.

Waterman, Robert. 1990. *Adhocracy: The Power to Change*. Knoxville, TN: Whittle Direct Books.

Weber, George. 1971. "Inner City School Children Can Be Taught to Read: Four Successful Schools." Occassional Paper 18, Council for Basic Education, Washington, D.C.

Why Do Some Schools Succeed? 1980. Bloomington, IN: Phi Delta Kappa.

About *Creating the New American School* and the National Educational Service

The mission of the National Educational Service is to help create environments in which **all** children and youth will succeed. *Creating the New American School* is just one of many resources and staff development opportunities we provide that focus on building a **Community Circle of Caring**™. If you have any questions, comments, articles, manuscripts, or youth art you would like us to consider for publication, please contact us at the address below.

Staff Development Opportunities Include:

Discipline with Dignity
Managing Disruptive Behavior
Ensuring Safe Schools
Improving Schools through Quality Leadership
Integrating Technology Effectively
Creating Professional Learning Communities
Building Cultural Bridges
Reclaiming Youth At Risk
Working with Today's Families

National Educational Service
1252 Loesch Road, PO Box 8
Bloomington, IN 47402
(812) 336-7700
(800) 733-6786
FAX (812) 336-7790
e-mail: nes@nes.org
WWW: http://www.nes.org/

NEED MORE COPIES OR ADDITIONAL RESOURCES ON THIS TOPIC?

Need more copies of this book? Want your own copy? Need additional resources on this topic? If so, you can order additional materials by using this form or by calling us at (800) 733-6786 or (812) 336-7700. Or you can order by FAX at (812) 336-7790.

Preview any resource for 30 days without obligation. If you are not completely satisfied, simply return it within 30 days of receiving it and owe nothing.

°Title	Price	Quantity	Total
Creating the New American School	$19.95		
Beyond Piecemeal Improvements	$21.95		
Cooperative Classroom	$19.95		
Creating Learning Communities: The Role of the Teacher in the 21st Century	$18.95		
How Can We Create Thinkers? Questioning Strategies that Work	$22.95		
How Smart Schools Get and Keep Community Support	$19.95		
Leading Schools to Quality (video and leader's guide)	$250.00		
Parents Assuring Student Success	$21.95		
Principal As Staff Developer	$16.95		
School Based Management	$21.95		
Sharing Thinking Strategies	$22.95		
Teaching Students to Think	$21.95		
Shipping & Handling: Please add 7% of order total, or a minimum of $3.00, if check or credit card information is not enclosed.			

TOTAL _____

❑ Check enclosed with order ❑ Please bill me (P.O. #_____)
❑ VISA or MasterCard ❑ Money Order

Credit Card No._____ Exp. Date _____
Cardholder Signature _____

SHIP TO:
Name_____ Title _____
Organization _____
Address _____
City_____ State_____ ZIP _____
Phone_____ FAX _____

MAIL TO:
National Educational Service
1252 Loesch Road
P.O. Box 8
Bloomington, IN 47402